Official Know-It-All Guide™

ADVANCED MAGIC

Your Absolute, Quintessential, All You Wanted To Know, Complete Guide

Walter B. Gibson

Frederick Fell Publishers, Inc.

Fell's Official Know-It-All Guide to Advanced Magic
FREDERICK FELL PUBLISHERS, INC.

2131 Hollywood Boulevard
Hollywood, Florida 33020
800-771-3355
e-mail: fellpub@aol.com

Visit our web site at www.fellpub.com

Library of Congress Cataloging-in-Publication Data
Gibson, Walter B., 1897-
    Advanced Magic: your absolute, quintessential, all you wanted to know, complete guide to advanced magic / Walter B. Gibson; Ellia Chesnoff contributing editor.
       p. cm. -- (Fell's official know-it-all guide)
   ISBN 0-88391-017-9
   1. Magic tricks. I. Chessnoff, Ellia. II. Gibson, Walter Brown, 1897-Mastering magic
III. Title IV. Series.

GV1547 .G5175 2000
793.8--dc21
                                          99-016291

10 9 8 7 6 5 4 3 2 1
Copyright © 2000. All rights reserved.
Interior Design by Harry Rosenzweig

Table of Contents

PART 1

Close-Up Magic

PART 2

Card Tricks

PART 3

Stage Magic

PART 4

Mysticism & Mentalism

PART 5

Grand Illusion

PART 6

Historical Magic

Detailed Table of Contents

Introduction

Part 1: Close-Up Magic

PART 2: Card Tricks

PART 3: Stage Magic

Part 4: Mysticism and Mentalism

Part 5: Grand Illusion

Part 6: Historical Magic

Foreword

As long as there is Magic, Walter B. Gibson will remain a part of it. He was a prolific writer of books and magazines about magic. From historic books on Harry Houdini to the best teaching books on magic, Walter could write it all. He was the ghost-writer behind Houdini, Howard Thurston, Harry Blackstone, and Joseph Duninger, to name but a few. No other author has contributed as much to magic as Gibson.

No one loved writing more than Walter. In his lifetime he wrote over three hundred novels and fifteen hundred publications, although not all of them were in his name. He used "Maxwell Grant" for his very famous radio series, "The Shadow." There is not a library of consequence that will not have some of his novels and magic books on hand.

Over the years, Walter invented many top-selling magic tricks and most of them are still being sold today. Some of his popular ones are "Nickels to Dimes", "The Double Bill Tube", and "Oil and Water".

He certainly served as an inspiration to thousands of professional magicians and countless amateurs who learned magic from Walter's books. From 1927, when he wrote "The World's Best Book on Magic," to 1981 when he wrote " Walter Gibson's Big Book on Magic for All Ages," he managed to pass his keen magical knowledge to others. He also has been the source for inventors who have used his books and magazines as a source for their tricks.

To learn magic you must start with a good teaching book, and Walter's *Mastering Magic* is the best you could find! This is a general book on magic that teaches how to perform tricks, gives some insight into the lives of the master magicians and provides ideas on showmanship. It also provides you the secrets behind many other magic tricks and big stage illusions of past and present. Although this book was written years ago, many of the elements of magic have not changed. The principles are as current today as when they were first written. In this printing, the original ideas are expanded and brought up to date. New illustrations have been added to make it easier for you to learn the tricks.

A list of U.S. and Canada magic dealers—including names, addresses and pone numbers—are made available following Chapter 8. You can call or write to them for a free catalog or visit those in your hometown.

With the use of this book you will be amazing your friends and relatives with ease, as you go from trick to trick, showing off your new-found skill. You will be rewarded with smiles, applause and friendships.

When I was in my teens, I read my first Gibson book. The years have passed and now I'm over 50. My profession is inventing magic tricks, marketing, lecturing, and performing them. It has taken me all over the world. Magic is a universal language. Even when I was unable to utter a word of the language in the country I was visiting, I was still able to communicate and entertain with magic. Since magic is so visual no words were necessary.

I still use some tricks that I learned when I read my first Walter Gibson book. I am sure you, too, will find tricks from this master that you will be performing for many years.

Just as Walter wrote in "The Shadow," "The week of crime bears bitter fruit"; he could have written "the rewards of magic bears the sweetest fruit."

Contributing Editor Biography

Elia Ilan Chesnoff, like many of the great entertainers, started off as a juggler. From juggling he was introduced to magic when his sisters bought him a simple magic set. After reading every magic book he could get his hands on, four or five times over, his knowledge of tricks became as well known as that of any old time magician. At age twelve he started performing at children's birthday parties where he struggled for two years before he pulled off a successful show. It wasn't until he met South Florida's leading illusionist and master magician, Gary Lightinheart, that he learned the secrets to the art of **PERFORMING** magic. Gary Lightinheart became his mentor, guide, and long time friend.

For the past 11 years Elia has performed throughout Florida. From his close-up magic to his illusion shows, Elia manages to sneak into the hearts of all who experience his magic – filling them with fantasy and wonder. He show-cased several times at the University of Florida, where he also received a bachelor's degree in English and a Master's degree in Education. Elia has also developed courses that are dedicated to teaching magic in several summer camps and after school programs.

His experience with education combined with his knowledge of magic make him the perfect product for teaching this secret art. But in revising this book he successfully brought the relationship of the mentor and student onto the page so that everyone who reads this book can understand how magic has been learned and mastered for centuries; where secrets are passed down from a master to an apprentice.

Introduction

I feel the difference between those who do tricks and those who perform magic will be most noticeable by how they view the information in the introduction. The amateur magician might skim through the introduction briefly out of curiosity but jump to and concentrate on the effects. A common thought that jumps into their mind might be *every magic book starts off by telling the reader to practice and never reveal the secrets blah blah blah.* They will value the technical secrets to each effect and like a sponge soak up the knowledge of how every trick is done. The artists of magic will value the introduction because they understand the difference between knowing how a trick is done and being able to perform it – the latter being where the real secret in magic lies. This introduction discusses some of the concepts that turn tricks into memorable magical moments.

It's All About The Audience

I start off discussing the audience because they are the most important factor in your magic being successful. They can appreciate your skills with applause and laughter or they can debunk your deceptions like a sinister wild mob chanting "Burn the fraud!" The point is that nobody likes to be duped. Everybody enjoys being entertained. This was perhaps the most important lesson I learned from my mentor Gary Lightinheart. He mesmerized his audience by making them feel comfortable, by welcoming them into his home of wonder, and sharing with them the enjoyment of feasting on fantasy. He leaves his audiences grateful to him for taking them on a magical experience.

On the other hand I've seen too many magicians who are only about outsmarting their audience to boost their own ego. They will bring up a volunteer and make a fool out of them, perhaps because they lack in self-confidence and this is how they deal with their insecurities. The audience ends up laughing because they are scared that if they don't the magician will pick on them next. Meanwhile the volunteer stands up on stage with a worried smile hoping the trick ends as soon as possible. It's an awful sight. Unfortunately there are many of these types of magicians out there because magic welcomes these types of egotists. For them the magic comes down to being able to say, in a much more eloquent way, "Na Na boo boo, I know something you don't know." Go to any magic club meeting and you're bound to run into a dozen or so of these type of people. Beware of falling into their trap and becoming the same way.

Why entertain your audience? That's what they really want! A great example of this is when you look at two jugglers Zach and Timmy. Timmy can juggle five torches in one hand on a six foot unicycle while blindfolded. The audience watches this for ten seconds amazed beyond belief. Then they get bored and walk away. Zach balances a small kids chair on his chin and keeps the audience spell bound for five minutes. How does he do it. He talks to the audience and makes jokes. He has people inspect the chair. He brings volunteers up on stage to lay down in front of him as he balance the chair over them. He pretends to have trouble balancing the chair. He builds suspense and just at the moment of tension he succeeds not only in balancing the chair but keeping the audience amused for a lengthy period of time. This principle works with magic. Milk your tricks. Mooo! But be careful of overdoing it because this will annoy your audience and bore them as well. The right balance will leave them wanting more.

How to choose volunteers can be critical in making your effect successful. An uncooperative volunteer can ruin your trick. A silly person can bring your audience into an uproar which only makes you the entertainer look that much better. So don't pick people who you might think will upstage you or try to compete with you. Choose volunteers who want to have a good time and most important are competent and respectful. How can you tell which audience members will be good volunteers? Look for the people who are allowing themselves to be awed. Look for the people who are laughing and enjoying themselves. Then bring that person up on stage and make them look good. Play with them. Joke with them, but **do not** embarrass them. Have fun with your new assistant. This will cause more audience members to want to volunteer. Remember that making a volunteer look good makes you look good.

Condition your audience so that they can suspend their will to disbelieve. The magic happens in the audience's mind not in your hands. It is in the mind of the audience where they take a suggestion (perhaps that you are floating a match) and make it real for themselves. To create this magic mood do what I've already told you. **Entertain** your audience. Let them know that you aren't here to trick them but rather to provide them with the fun and joy of imagining if what you are doing is actually real.

I found that entertaining and getting the audience on my side resolved any issues or problems I had with audience management. If you still, although unlikely, get a heckler. The best thing to do is ignore the person and not stoop down to their level. I've had audiences defend me and heckle the heckler before. Remember the audience wants you to succeed and if you entertain them, you have.

<u>The Element Of Surprise: Why We Don't Show Tricks Twice</u>

The best way to explain this principle is in a little demonstration. In the picture, I have five cards. Choose one of them, but don't tell me which one it is.

Now I'm going to make one of the cards disappear. As I'm making the card disappear I want you to focus on the card that you chose. Imagine the card that you chose is being chewed up in my mouth. Imagine your card vanishing into the acids in my stomach.

Isn't it amazing that the card you chose has vanished. Try doing this trick a few more times and I bet you'll figure out how it works.

The fact that the audience does not know what to expect can become extremely useful to the magician. More often than not, watching a trick numerous times will reveal the secret. If the magician surprises you by making a red ball appear under a cup, it is because you weren't expecting it. If he does the same trick for you, you'll be looking for the red ball and ignoring everything else. Because most of the secrets of magic are subtle, multiple performances of a trick allow for the audience to pick up those subtleties.

I can guarantee you that if you show a spectator a good trick they will ask to see it again and again. You have a few options to deal with this. **Option 1**: Have a follow-up trick and tell them "Okay, but first let me show you a different trick." By the time you finish your follow up trick the person might forget that they asked you to repeat the first trick. If they do ask you to repeat the first trick, tell them sorry you just ran out of time and you have to go. Or make up some other bologna excuse. **Option 2**: End your effects with something silly or make a joke that will make the audience forget to ask you to repeat the effect. **Option 3:** Repeat the trick when asked but have a different surprise ending. This is extremely popular among magicians, often referred to as the double wammy, because you are not only fulfilling their request but you are further mystifying your audience. Sometimes repeating a trick can be used to your advantage because you have planted the expectations in your audience's minds.

Along with not repeating a trick I'd like to mention that you should, when performing magic, quit while you are ahead. Once you have entertained your audience and wowed them, "Speaking words of wisdom, let it be." Leaving your audience wanting more is a good rule to practice because it ultimately leaves you and them satisfied. Going past your limit is like over eating, you suddenly feel nauseous and are sitting on the toilet wishing you hadn't done it.

Practicing, Though Hassling, Makes The Magic Fascinating

Lance Burton walked out on stage wearing the classic black tux with tales and said to the audience, "Every three years there is an International competition in magic." He tried saying it in French – the way it's supposed to be pronounced. "I know French sounds funny with a southern accent. It's like the Olympics of magic. I was the first American to bring back the gold. So, I thought you might like to see that act." He said this in the most humble way he could. The audience applauded and he said, "I'm glad you feel that way." The lights dimmed and a female assistant brought him a cane and top hat. Behind him there was an old-fashioned lamppost like the kind Gene Kelly danced around in <u>Singing in the Rain</u>. The melodic music began.

After lighting the top of the cane with his cigarette, a flash of fire slowly traveled across the cane to his hand. He held the flame there for a second and closed his hand to throw the flame out to the audience but a pure white dove flew out instead. The audience applauded as Lance Burton bowed in his elegant fashion holding the cane and hat. He perched the bird on his cane and let it fly from the cane to the top of the lamppost. All of his movements were slow and deliberate.

He removed his gloves and folded them over each other making a white bundle. He threw the bundle toward the audience where, in mid air, it turned into a dove which flew to the end of the stage and then back to his hand. From his fingers the dove flew to his head instead of the lamppost. He took the bird off his head and shook his index finger at it as if reprimanding the dove for misbehaving. The mistake was acknowledged when the magician shrugged his shoulders, smiled, and let the dove fly back to the lamppost. The mistake added to the act by making Lance seem more human.

He rolled up his jacket- and shirt- sleeves to eliminate our suspicion and pulled a white silk scarf off his neck. After running the scarf through his fingers a few times to show that it was empty he produced a white candle from underneath and in one continuous movement pulled a lit match from behind his lapel to light the candle. The audience applauded which made him smile. The more complicated his sleight of hand seemed the slower his movements became. He threw the scarf over his left shoulder and held the candle in his right hand. His other hand grabbed the flame off the candle making it flash and the candle disappeared.

Lance Burton made the candle reappear under the silk. Holding the scarf in his left hand he ran it through the fingers of his right hand and pulled out two more white candles. He displayed the three candles in his left hand and smiled at the audience. He blew out two of the candles and dropped them into a box that was in front of the lamppost. He wrapped the scarf around the third candle, gave the scarf a tug making the candle disappear, and bundled up the scarf to produce a dove. Lance was as smooth as the silk scarf that the dove was fluttering its wings over. The audience applauded.

He threw the scarf into the box and kept the dove perched on his fingers. He walked to the front of the stage, grabbed the bird and threw it into the air where it turned into the white scarf which fell as slow as a feather. He caught it and put it around his neck the same way it was when he started his routine. It was a sign of completion. He bowed as the mesmerized audience clapped and cheered. Then he said, "Thank you. You've just witnessed twenty years of my life in a minute and 30 seconds."

I tell you this little story to stress the point of practicing. As in any other art you must practice to master it. A wise guru once told me, "the better you get, the more you practice." One of the most difficult things to do is learn a new trick and then not show it to someone immediately. I'm guilty of it as much as the next magician. We must work hard to control this unexplainable force that suddenly overcomes us and makes us perform a trick before we are ready. I believe that practicing is not only beneficial because it allows for you to master a sleight, but even more important it allows for you to relax while you are performing. There is nothing worse than watching a nervous performer. This is because deep down the audience really wants the performer to succeed. Practicing a trick makes the magician confident which then allows for the magician to relax. It is extremely noticeable to figure out when the magician is doing their secret move. Simply look for the sweat droplets forming on the brow, the sudden Stutter, and the jerky hand movements. Relaxing from practicing ameliorates this tense moment. If you are relaxed the audience will relax, and when they are relaxed those secret moves become much easier to pull off.

Master Magicians Master Misdirection

Misdirection can be defined as forcing an audience's focus so they do not see your secret move which allows for the magic to happen. A common myth that is dispersed among magicians and layman is that sleight of hand is the most powerful tool for magicians. I'm sure you've heard the expression *the hand is faster than the eye*. This expression was probably invented by magicians because they did not want anyone to learn the real tool magician's use – misdirection.

The best way I can think of explaining the power of misdirection is in the story of the oreo cookie thief. This story takes me back to college my sophomore year while living in the dorms. A few of my buddies from the floor congregated in my room to shoot the sh... breeze. Then this guy named Harris walked in. Harris is one of these guys who loves to hear his own voice. He's like a verbal spider who will trap any innocent bystander into his conversational web. He crawled into my room and joined, I mean dominated, our conversation.

Like the good host momma trained me to be, I provided everyone with some food. I gave each of my five guests three oreo cookies. That's a combined total of fifteen oreo cookies. But I was feeling generous and gregarious that evening. Apparently my generosity was not enough for Harris. While Harris was talking, which often involved fluid hand movement, he had one of his hands reach over into my stash of oreo cookies and swipe two additional cookies. All the while acting relaxed as the dexterity of his finger palmed two more cookies and he even went as far as to swing the cookies around as if they were a natural part of his visual speaking hands. I must admit his sleight of hand and sense of relaxation were impressive, but I caught him. He wasn't going to get away with it. That's right I called him on it. You better think twice before stealing my cookies mister.

I later thought about why, even with his incredible ability of prestidigitation, he got caught swiping the cookies. At that moment I had the epiphany that misdirection is more powerful than sleight of hand. If I wanted to swipe his cookies I would have used misdirection. In the same scenario I would have had two accomplices outside the room create a big commotion. Maybe they'd get into a food fight – that always attracts a crowd. While everybody is misdirected because they all go outside the room to check out the food fight, I would swipe four cookies (2 for myself, and 1 for each of my accomplices). I realized that I could do a sloppy job in swiping the cookies and still not get caught.

This is how I realized that misdirection was more powerful than sleight of hand. I mean in no way to discredit sleight of hand, but rather to show that powerful sleight of hand combined with misdirection can create some of the most powerful effects in magic.

Reviewing the Magic Principles
1. Respect and entertain your audience.
2. Never do a trick twice unless you've got a double wammy and always leave the audience wanting more.
3. Magic is 2 percent of audience fascination, and 98 percent magician's perspiration. So get practicing to avoid perspiration during performance.
4. Misdirection + Sleight of Hand = free oreo cookies.

Part I
Close-Up Magic

Close-up magic encompasses any magical effect that is done for a few people, up close and personal. Many magicians specialize only in close-up magic. They often work restaurants and the tables at private affairs. There are a few close-up artists who have made a name for themselves by working behind a bar. Even in Copperfield's grand shows he always tries to fit some close-up magic into his act. It should be no surprise that close-up magic is so popular when the audience relies mainly on sight as the judge for what they believe or disbelieve.

This chapter is divided into two sections: Puzzles and Pocket Tricks. Both sections are filled with effects that are perfect for performing at a restaurant while waiting for food or for bringing life to a mundane party. Most magicians start by learning close-up magic because the tricks are fairly small and therefore convenient. I recommend that you read through this chapter and choose a few of the effects to master, and I mean **master.** Once you have mastered them and perhaps become bored with performing the same effects, then move on to some new ones. There is a saying in magic, "It is better to perform two or three effects well, than fifteen effects poorly."

Section 1: Magic Puzzles and Games

It is wise to begin with tricks that puzzle rather than mystify, dealing in stunts more than magic. Anything that intrigues an audience is good entertainment. If it baffles, so much the better, and if the idea itself is ingenious, people will still appreciate it if they do catch on. By following one baffling stunt with another, the performer can cause the onlookers to lose the thread of things and often to forget something which they thought they knew.

This Section is therefore dedicated to such devices—a whole collection of them.

Admittedly, some of this close-up magic is derived from puzzles, but falls distinctly in the magical category. One great dividing line between a puzzle and a trick is that the secret of a puzzle lies in the answer and must therefore be revealed; whereas the secret of a trick need never be explained. In other terms, a trick is demonstrable whereas a puzzle is only explanatory. Close-up magic used to be called "Twizzlers." The term "Twizzler" has been coined to represent a puzzle or paradox which can be demonstrated. Seeing it accomplished, people will still have to guess the how or wherefore. That gives the Twizzler the status of a trick, which in turn introduces the element of Magic.

All these Twizzlers are intended for impromptu performance, which is the accepted way of testing ones magical aptitudes. Common objects are used and while various suggestions are made, the individual performer does not have to limit himself to those described. The basic facts thus established, the next step is to introduce the Twizzlers.

1. Coin and Saucer

This one is a "giveaway," but it presents such a seemingly impossible problem that it will always command interest.

The Puzzle:
The performer opens proceedings by dropping a coin into a saucer, then pouring the contents of a half-filled glass of water into the saucer, so the coin is submerged. The trick is to remove the coin from the saucer without getting the fingers wet. No one is allowed to touch the saucer. To make it all the harder, the water must remain in the saucer after the coin is removed.

Method:
The method is quite ingenious. Light a small quantity of paper and drop it, burning, into the glass. As the paper finishes burning, invert the glass on the saucer, not over the coin but alongside it. Hold the inverted glass slightly tilted and the water will surge up into the glass. Let the glass rest upside down in the saucer, the glass Detaining the water. The coin may then be picked up without wetting the fingers.

As soon as the coin is removed from the saucer the glass is lifted and the water escapes down into the saucer again.

Younger children should not try this effect without adult supervision.

2. Toothpick Field Goal

This puzzle is great for when you're at a restaurant and the food is taking just a little too long to get to the table. It's also great for when you're out to eat with some friends and the conversation comes to a halt. It's even fun to do when the conversation doesn't come to a halt. Try it.

The Puzzle:
Set up four toothpicks so they look like a football field goal. Then ball up a little piece of paper, or use a penny, and stick it in the field goal. Tell your spectators that the object is to rearrange the toothpicks so that the paper ball is not in the field goal. Not to difficult right? The catch is that you are only allowed to move two of the toothpicks. Now sit back and enjoy people argue and strategize for the next fifteen minutes about how to accomplish this simply deceptive task. The funniest thing to look for, and there is always one of these people in the group, is when one person starts yelling in excitement, "I've got it. I've got it. Wait. Wait. Here it is." Then they begin to try it and fail falling flat on their face, swearing that they had figured out the puzzle.

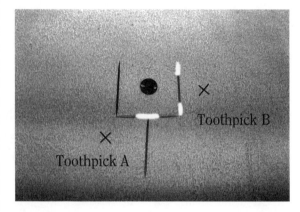

3

Method:
In order to make it simpler for you to understand how this trick works I have marked the two toothpicks that are to be rearranged. Slide the toothpick with the black stripe in the center (toothpick A) over to the left so that the left goal post is centered perpendicular to the toothpick.

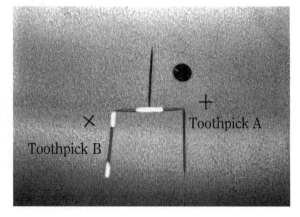

Then move the toothpick with the white stripes on the end so that it is across from the original bottom toothpick.

I recommend that you practice this trick and make sure you do it well because it is one of these puzzles that suddenly becomes very hard to do, even if you know how it's done, when you are under pressure. There is nothing worse than putting a puzzle out their on the table and then not being able to show your spectators that it can actually be done. Riots have been started for less.

3. The Tom Cruise Match Trick

This is not really a puzzle or a trick, but rather a cool juggling stunt that is bound to make you popular among the pyromaniac crowd. If you've ever seen the movie *Cocktail* then you know what I'm talking about.

Effect: In the movie, Tom Cruise plays a bartender with masterful juggling skills. At one point he lights a match with one hand and throws it across the bar so a woman can light her cigarette.

4

Method: If you know how to snap than you will have no problem learning how to pull off this skillful stunt. You stick your index finger into a book of matches and open up the flap (So far pretty easy). Then bend one of the matches completely over the bottom of the matchbook so that the head of the match is against the striker. Place the middle finger over the head of the match pressing it to the striker with the thumb underneath the matchbook. You should be in a position to snap your

fingers. At this point simply snap your fingers and the match should light as the matchbook flies across the table or bar with the lit match sticking up. It might take a little practice until you get it right. As a magician I'm over protective about my fingers. With that in mind I always quickly lick my middle finger before attempting this juggling fire feat to avoid any possible burns.

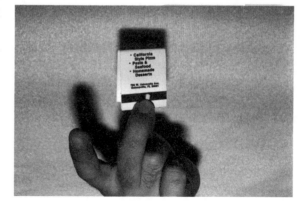

I once read a book on fire eating. The first part of the book went into a lengthy discussion about liability in which the author takes no responsibility for the readers' health when attempting the pyro feats. I didn't even read the remainder of the book let alone try any of the fire feats. I'm taking this paragraph and using it in the same way to remind you that if you do get burned I'm not responsible and you better read how to do the effect a bit more carefully.

But this effect is pretty safe, for the most part. Have fun and enjoy!

4. Match in Mid-air

Effect: A match is held between the tips of the thumbs and the fingers of both hands are locked in front of it. The thumbs are raised and the match mysteriously floats in mid-air behind the interlaced hands, the head of the match showing above the hands. Finally the thumbs are lowered and recapture the match between their tips. The fingers are then spread to show the hands quite empty.

Method: In taking the match originally, hold it between the thumb and second finger of the right hand, which enables the thumb to press the match under the nail of the finger, holding it upright. As the hands are brought together, that finger is kept folded inward, so that only seven fingers—not eight—are interlocked. The second finger of the left hand fills the space where the right second finger should be.

The thumbs are raised and the bent finger moves the match back and forth, producing the floating effect behind the screening fingers. Later, the tips of the thumbs are brought together to press the sides of the match, which allows the fingers to be drawn wide. No one will notice the absence of one finger from the interlocked hands.

While the trick can be performed with a lighted match, it is inadvisable except after long practice. With an unlighted match, there is plenty of time to set it in position and the trick can be continued longer. A large wooden match is the best to use, as the head will be seen more plainly and the hands will not have to be tilted forward, hence there is no chance of anyone spying the hidden finger. You can replace the match with a pencil or wand, to avoid playing with fire.

5. Drop the Match-Box

Effect: This is a tantalizing stunt that will often cause people to remain baffled without knowing why. Taking a box of safety matches, you hold it several inches above the table and drop it end downward. The box lands and remains standing on the table.

After a few such demonstrations, you invite others to try it, all dropping the box from the same height. They find that the box invariably bounces and falls over. Apparently, you alone have the knack of dropping the box just right.

Method: There's more to it than just the knack. In holding the box upright, take it at the top end, between the tips of the thumb and fingers. In so doing, use the other hand to push the drawer open, sliding it behind the screening fingers of the upper hand.

When the box is dropped it has a tendency to bounce when it strikes. But the drawer, sliding downward and shut from the impact, provides the needed stability to keep the box upright. It shuts so suddenly that no one realizes it was open when you dropped it.

Be sure to have the box fairly well filled with matches to give it weight. The drawer should be a loose one that will clamp shut rapidly. It is also wise to experiment beforehand to ascertain the maximum height from which you can drop the box and have it remain upright. The longer the drop, the more effective the trick and the less chance of some one else accidentally causing the box to stand.

6. Card and Glass

Effect: Balancing a plastic drinking glass (just in case you drop it) on the top edge of a playing card appears to be very difficult. Nevertheless, it can be learned with very brief practice, provided you know the trick that goes with it.

Method: Hold the card upright, thumb at one side, fingers at the other, with the exception of the forefinger, which stays behind the card. Using the other hand to set the glass on the edge of the card, raise the hidden forefinger so that it serves as a prop. The plastic glass should be set so that its center is slightly to the rear of the card, making it all the easier.

The lighter the plastic glass, the better. After a few trials, the balance can be done in convincing style, but it is most effective to make it look like a delicate, difficult job.

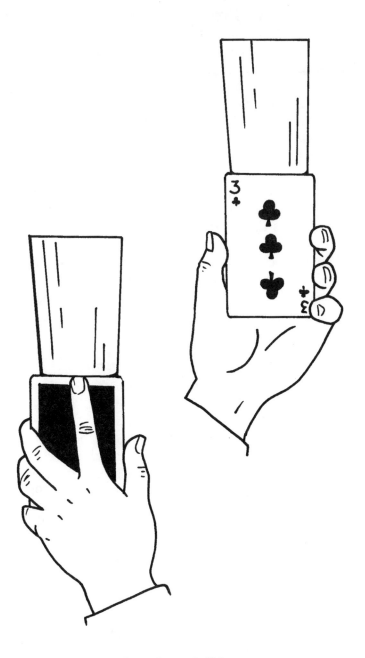

Card and Glass

7. Power of Thought

The Effect: Have a person hold a penny in one hand and a nickel in the other, without telling which is which. Then state: "I want you to multiply the coin in your left hand by two. You have it? Good. Now multiply the coin in your right hand by thirteen...Have you got it?" After the person nods, you tell him which hand holds the penny and which hand has the nickel, yet at no time has he declared the results of his multiplications.

Method: Though this is chiefly a "catch" it will often leave people baffled. The cue is the speed with which the person responds to the final question "Have you got it?" Only a brief pause should be made before springing that question. If the victim is holding the penny in his right hand, his multiplication of one times thirteen is almost instantaneous and he nods with it. But if the right hand holds the nickel, he will hesitate before he nods. This tells you which coin is in the right hand.

A more subtle version can be worked with a dime and a nickel. In this case, have the person multiply the left hand coin by five, the right-hand coin by seventeen. He'll get the dime total quickly by simply adding a zero as the multiple of ten, but will hesitate if he is multiplying 5 by 17.

8

8. Slapping Coins

Effect: This little close-up effect, although quite simple, has proven to be quite impressive for people. You hold to coins in the right hand. Both hands are held palms up above a table. You quickly turn over both hands simultaneously and slap them against the table. When you lift up your hands you can show that one of the coins from the right hand has jumped to the left hand.

Method:
The secret of this stunt lies in the placement of the coins in the two hands. Place the coins in the right palm, one under the pinkie and ring finger, while the other coin is placed beneath the pointer and middle finger. The natural motion of flipping your hands over and slapping them on the table thrusts the coin under the middle and pointer finger toward the left hand. The left hand should catch the coin as it flips over and slaps the table. With a little practice you'll get the timing down.
If you'd like to take this feat a step further you can add more coins by stacking them above the other two. While playing around one day I figured out a way to do this

effect with out a table by using one coin. I place a coin in the right palm and turn over my hands into a fist and cross them over each other. Then ask someone to choose the hand they saw the coin in and show them that the right hand is empty and the coin is actually in the left hand. This is accomplished by simply dropping the coin into the left hand as the right hand crosses over the left. This is one of those instances in magic when a larger movement hides a smaller movement.

9. What does a One handed knot and cherry stem have in common?

Effect: The magician holds the two ends of a rope in one hand. By dropping one of the ends and twirling the rope, the magician manages to put a knot into the end of the rope. Then the magician hands out the rope and challenges others to attempt this skillful feat.

Method: The irony about this puzzle is that the only skill that the magician needs to have is acting. A knot is pre-tied into one end of the rope. The knot is hidden in the fist of the hand holding the rope. Take the other end of the rope and place it in the same hand and then drop the un-knotted end while dramatically twirling the rope. The purpose of failing at the first or even second attempt of this trick is to condition the audience into believing that you are legitimately trying to put a knot into the rope with one hand.

9

This is where your acting skills come in. Be subtle about messing up. Act surprised that it didn't work and then make a joke out of it by saying, "The rope just needed to get warmed up." Or you might say something like, "Wow, I've never done that before. I not only put a knot into the rope but I also untied it so quickly that it couldn't even be seen." Then place the unknotted end of the rope back into your hand holding the knotted end. This time drop and twirl the pre-knotted end to show everyone you successfully completed the feat. Then undo the knot and pass the rope out and let the spectators try.

A nice version of this trick can be done at restaurants using your mouth to tie a cherry stem. Pre-tie a knot into the stem and have your index finger and thumb cover the knot when you hold it. Place the stem into your mouth, begin acting and viola' – show your fellow diner's how easy it is for you to put a knot into a stem.

I've known people to use this cherry stem trick as a scam into getting a free dinner. You put a bet out on the table that the first person to put a knot into the stem gets their dinner paid for by the other diners. Although, it seems a bit suspicious when you come up with the bet and then win. To do the scam properly you have to have an accomplice suggest the game (an accomplice can typically be bribed by offering to buy them dessert).

10. Coin and Bottle

Effect: A coin is placed on a table; a soda bottle is inverted and balanced upon the coin. The trick is to remove the bottle from the coin without touching either of the two objects. The bottle must be kept in its present upside-down position.

Method: This sounds close to impossible, but the stunt is actually quite easy, though it must be done neatly. Punch the table lightly and repeatedly with downward strokes of the fist. The bottle will jiggle itself over the edge of the coin and on to the table, still maintaining its balance.

Some practice is needed to work the stunt effectively. The bottle must not be jarred too heavily as it jiggles from the coin edge. Keeping it in slow but constant motion is the best process.

11. Knives and Glasses: The Art Piece

Effect: Three cups are placed on a table so that they create the corners of a triangle. Three knives are placed on the ends of the cups so that the tips meet in the center of the triangle. Finally, a cup is placed on top of the area where the three knives meet.

Method: This is neither a trick or a puzzle, but rather a neat balancing act to do at the end of a meal. It provides entertainment for not only you but it also spices up the mundane evening of a busboy. The secret to this balancing act is in how you lay the knives over each other at the center of the triangle. Each knife goes over and under another knife at the point where the centers meet. It's sort of hard to explain and the best way to figure it out is by matching up your knives with the knives in the picture.

12. Catch the Sugar

Effect: This is one of those feats that "can't be done" until you proceed to do it. The required articles are two lumps of sugar and a small drinking glass or cup that can almost be encircled by the thumb and fingers.

Have someone gird his hand about the glass and hold ,a lump of sugar between the tips of the thumb and finger. The second lump is then set on the first. The trick is to flip the upper lump into the glass, then do the same with the lower, so that both lumps are in the glass.

The first lump proves easy. A mere toss and it can be caught in the glass. But every time the remaining lump is tossed, the first one flies out of the glass. That's why everyone thinks it is impossible.

Method: Here's how you do it. Instead of tossing the second lump, hold the hand high, release the lump and drop the hand down with it. By sweeping the hand a little faster, you can bring the glass beneath the falling lump before it reaches the floor and thus catch it in the glass along with the first lump.
It takes some knack, as too rapid a swing may cause the first lump to leave the glass, but once acquired it is worth the trouble as it proves a very neat trick.

11

13. The Puzzling Label

Effect: This is more of a novelty than a trick; but it usually proves itself quite a puzzler. Picking up a bottle from among, some empties, you apparently discover something very curious about it: namely, that this bottle has its label on the inside instead of the outside. How that could have come about is something of a mystery.

Method: The bottle is fixed beforehand and planted along with the others to be picked out at an appropriate time. First, a label is soaked from a bottle, then rolled about a pencil. The bottle it partly filled with water and laid on its side. The label is slid from the pencil and pushed into the bottle where it unrolls as it floats on the water.

Gradually shake the water from the bottle, letting the label settle toward the lower side, where it is easily guided to the required position. The label attaches itself to the inside of the bottle, remaining there for later display.

Section 2: Pocket Magic

There was a time when professional magicians confined nearly all their legerdemain to the stage, and amateur wizards were wont to copy their example. But as more and more persons took up the art as a hobby, it became the custom to perform magic on call. Any one performing magic for his friends could hardly beg off because he had no equipment handy, so there came a demand for pocket tricks, which today represent the most thriving branch of the business.

Pocket magic has been given the professional touch by Blackstone, whose skill at performing amazing close-up mysteries has set the pace for other magicians. Years ago, Herrmann used to perform odd feats of wizardry at the stage door or in the hotel dining room, finding that such marvels attracted people to the theater. Today, magic is often presented so informally that a performer must constantly be ready with some impromptu surprise.

Various pocket tricks can be performed with ordinary articles, so this chapter contains some items of that type. There is a constant increase, however, in pocket tricks that are done with special appliances, some of which can be prepared or constructed fairly easily, though there are many that need precision made devices obtainable through magical dealers.

12

Examples of this type are found in the present chapter, and will give the reader a better insight into ways and means of this fascinating branch of wizardry.

1. The Penetrating Match

Effect: This ingenious effect must both be seen and tested to appreciate its baffling effect. The appliances consist of a fair-sized safety pin and a large match, from which the head has been broken off cleanly, so that the two ends appear identical.

The point of the pin is worked through the center of the match, care being taken not to split the wood. The match is slid along to the middle of the pin which is then clasped. Thus the match is impaled upon the loose bar of the pin; whichever way it is revolved, its progress is halted by the solid bar of the pin.

The performer holds the ends of the pin firmly between the thumb and forefinger of each hand, with the solid bar downward. With the second finger of either hand, he swivels the match downward until it is blocked by the solid bar. With the same finger, he presses the lower end of the match hard against the solid bar, at the far side. He gives a quick, inward snap with his finger, so the finger clears the end of the match.

The snap brings the match right through the bar, the wood visibly penetrating the steel. Swiveling the match around again, the performer repeats the snap with the same amazing result. In order that people can observe the penetration more clearly, the performer folds a small piece of paper and hangs it on the bar. Another snap, and the match comes through both the paper and the bar.

Method: Properly practiced, the trick becomes amazingly effective, yet the method is extremely simple. When snapped, the match actually recoils from the pin, making a rapid revolution in a backward direction. This happens so swiftly that the eye cannot follow it. The result is an optical illusion of the match penetrating the pin.

The addition of the folded paper heightens the effect, serving as a background against which the action of the match can be better observed, yet still will carry the same illusion. Because of the reverse revolution, the ends of the match change places; this is the reason why the match head must be broken off and the ends made to appear the same.

2. Self-Opening Match-Box

13

Effect: A quick, effective pocket trick. Somebody wants a match, so the magician extends a box of matches and invites the person to take one. As the person reaches for the box, it suddenly opens and a few of the matches fly out into his hand.

Method: Take a rubber band and gird it around the sides and ends of the matchbox cover, lengthwise. Then push the drawer into the box, forcing in the rubber band like an inside loop. The rear of the box must be pressed firmly at top and bottom, between the thumb and forefinger, to hold the drawer.

Simply release the pressure at the right moment and the rubber band will shoot the drawer open so forcibly that some of the matches will fly out. With a light rubber band, the drawer will stop before it is clear of the box, so the magician simply pockets the box, then casually brings out an ordinary closed box in its place.

If a heavier band is used, the drawer will shoot clear and spill its matches on the table. In that case, there is plenty of opportunity to slip the rubber band from the cover and drop it unnoticed to the floor. The best box to use in the trick is a wooden safety-match box.

3. Self-Closing Match-Box

Effect: Here the magician extends a box of matches to a spectator, inviting him to take a match, since the box is open. As the person reaches for a match, the box shuts of its own accord. Much surprised, the magician pushes open the drawer again; offers a match to someone else. The provoking matchbox promptly snaps shut as it did before.

Method: A rubber band is the motivating force. It should be a thin band, dark in color, so that it is scarcely noticeable around the sides and ends of the box, where it is placed. When the drawer is pushed open, the rubber band stretches and is all the less likely to be seen. However, the matchbox should be kept constantly in motion during the course of the trick.

Encircle the box with the band and have it ready in the pocket. Push the drawer open and hold it open by pressing the top and bottom of the box at the back, between thumb and forefinger. Release the pressure and the box will shut. Push the drawer open and the trick is ready for a repeat. A wooden box of safety matches is the type to use.

This makes a good trick in combination with the "Self-Opening Match-Box." Two boxes can be shown, one in each hand. The box in the left hand is open; that in the right is closed. A wavy motion of the boxes toward each other and the box on the left goes shut, while the right-hand box opens at the same instant.

Some practice is needed to accomplish this effectively, as the boxes must be set before the trick, each hand helping the other to make ready.

4. The Rattling Match Boxes

Effect: The Magician pulls out an empty matchbox and a penny. The magician has one of the spectators sign the coin. Then the signed penny is placed inside the matchbox. The magician rattles the penny inside the box by one of the audience member's ears. He then brings out two more matchboxes, but leaves them empty. The magician then explains to the audience: "This is based on the old Pea and Shell game. You have to follow the matchbox with the coin in it. If you can follow the matchbox successfully after I've mixed them up, then you can keep the coin. Of course we'll just play for fun."

Two spectators are asked to play. One of them always chooses the correct box while the other always chooses the incorrect box. For a finally, the person who lost

14

has a chance to win big. Tell the spectator, "Okay, I feel bad that you keep on losing so I'm going to give you a chance to win five bucks. All you have to do is guess which box the coin is in just like before. To be fair I'll give you three chances." The magician moves the matchboxes around rattling the one with the coin in it and then has the spectator take three guesses. But the magician doesn't mix up the boxes between guesses and the spectator finds that none of the boxes contain the coin. The coin has disappeared and reappeared in the magician's pocket. The magician pulls the signed coin out of the pocket and has the spectators verify the signature.

Method: The effect involves some preparation. Start by taking a fourth match box with an extra penny inside and rubber banding it to your left arm underneath your shirt sleeve. Then cut a slit into the drawer component of one of the three matchboxes seen in the routine.

The slit should be just large enough for the penny to slide out of. First pull out the penny and have somebody sign it. While a spectator is signing the penny pull out the rigged matchbox (the matchbox with the slit in it) from your pocket. Open the drawer to show it is empty and then place the signed coin into the matchbox. Close the matchbox and rattle the coin inside. Then holding the matchbox in the right hand, tilt the matchbox so that the coin slides out of the slit and into the palm of the hand. While the coin is in the hand transfer the now empty matchbox to the left hand.

15

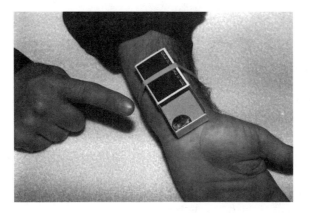

Simultaneously, as the left hand supposedly rattles the coin in the matchbox (the matchbox rubber banded to the arm is really making the sound), the right hand palming[1] the coin goes into the pocket where it dumps[2] the coin and brings out the two other empty matchboxes. Because you are pulling out two other match boxes from your pocket the audience will not find

it suspicious that your hand just went into the pocket and will thus never suspect the you have dumped the signed penny there – thus leaving you clean[3] for the remainder of the effect. Then depending on which person chooses which ever matchbox, use either the right or left hand to shake the box showing the spectator to either be correct or wrong. As a finally, show all the boxes empty and pull the signed coin from out of your pocket.

16

Tips:

• Keep the fourth matchbox rubber banded to your arm as close to the wrist as possible. This will make the rattling sound more convincing.
• When practicing this routine pay close attention to accidental rattling and make sure it's eliminated before you perform it.

[1]Palming - Secretly holding an object in the hand so that the audience thinks the hand is empty.
[2]Dump - When you secretly drop off an ovject that was in your hand that you supposedly made disappear.
[3]Clean - When you have finished a secret move and are free from getting caught

5. Four Coins and a Magic Mouth (magicians force)

Effect: The magician displays three different coins in his hand. In the other hand the magician holds a duplicate of one of the three coins concealed in his fist. The magician tells the audience, "I have made a prediction of which one of these coins will be chosen by the spectator. A duplicate of the coin is in my fist. Lets call this the prediction coin." The magician has a spectator choose a coin and then opens his fist to show the prediction to be correct.

Method: If you'll notice, the title is called *Four Coins and a Magic Mouth*, and the method of this trick is accomplished by the magic mouth. The principle behind this effect is called the magician's force[4]. The language in this effect is the method and must therefore be given special attention. Start by placing three coins in the left hand (lets say a quarter, dime, and penny). Then place a duplicate of one of those coins into the right hand (lets say it's the dime). Now you are ready to begin. The idea is to manipulate the volunteer into choosing the coin in your right fist (in this case the dime). Start by saying, "I have three coins in my left hand and a duplicate of one of these coins in my right hand. Lets call the duplicate coin the prediction coin. I have predicted that you will choose the coin that is in my right fist." Here comes the part where your language must be perfect: " Now, would you please pick up two of the coins from my left hand, one coin in each hand." Remember we are trying to force the spectator to choose the dime. At this point there are two possible scenarios.

The first scenario is that they can choose the quarter and the penny, leaving the dime in the left palm. If this should happen then the trick ends as you say, "You see I had the volunteer choose two of the coins thus eliminating them and leaving the coin that I predicted would be chosen." As you say this bring the two hands together and show the two dimes.

The second scenario is that the spectator will pick up the dime and one of the other coins. When this happens you place the coin not chosen in the left hand (either the quarter or penny) and place it on a table or into your pocket. Show your left palm empty and say "You have one coin in your left hand and one in your right hand. Will you please place one of those coins back into my left hand." If they place the dime back into your hand, open your fist while putting your hands together and

17

---

[4]Magicians Force - This is one of the most valued principles in magic in which the magician uses language to
        manipulate a volunteer into thinking they are choosing of their own free will one of any three
        objects while in actuality
        the magician is forcing the spectator to chose the desired object.

say "Isn't that just amazing. The coin you chose is the same as the prediction coin." If they give you the non-forced coin (either the quarter or penny) then place that coin either in your pocket or on a table as you did earlier. It is important that the movement be exactly as it was with the other non-forced coin because it creates a consistency in the spectators mind that suggests you perform this effect the same way each time. Then open your palm and bring it next to theirs and say, "It's amazing. I had you eliminate two of the coins and you are left with the same coin as I had predicted."

I know this trick seems rather silly. After reading the method you might even feel that you could not dupe anyone with it, but the magicians force is one of the most powerful magic principles and its success is solely based on your acting skills. This is clearly one of those tricks that you never perform twice for the same audience.

6. Turning a Penny into Two Quarters

Effect: The magician holds a penny in his hand between the thumb and forefinger. Instantaneously the penny turns into two quarters.

18

Method: This effect is simple but quite beautiful and baffling. It answers one of the most common questions I get as a magician, "Can you make my money multiply?" I answer, "Yes, 50 times over."

Hold the penny in your right hand between your thumb and forefinger. The two quarters are placed behind the penny so that they are perpendicular to the penny. The penny and fingers actually hide the two quarters. At this point you have probably figured out that your angles are of the utmost importance in creating this illusion. This should typically not be performed for more than two or three people at a time. Now that your setup is done and you are showing them the penny. Tell your spectators, "Okay, focus on Lincoln's ear, or nose, or beard, or tie. I bet that although you've handled thousands of pennies you have never really noticed some of those details." By giving the audience something specific to focus on, you are limiting their depth of field which will help in concealing the two quarters. At this point your left hand should momentarily cover the penny as your left thumb pushes the penny behind the quarters and revolves the quarters into view. Then hold one of the quarters in your left hand while the right hand holds the quarter with the penny behind it.

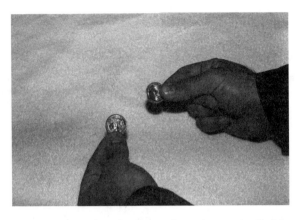

At this point show the two coins briefly and drop all three of them into your pocket. As you place the coins into your pocket your audience is bound to ask to inspect the coins. In order to distract them momentarily say something crazy like, "If you think that's impressive you should see me swallow coals and poop diamonds." Meanwhile palm[5] the penny from your pocket. Then say, "Your probably wondering what happened to the penny? Me too." Then pretend to sneeze into the hand palming the penny to create the illusion that you've sneezed a penny out of your nose.

7. Stack-the-Chips

Effect: This intriguing pocket trick is worked with a batch of poker chips or similar counters, which are embellished with large colored spots. Each chip has a spot on each side and in all cases the colors vary.

For instance, one chip has a red spot on one side, orange on the other. A second chip is labeled orange and yellow. Others are yellow and green; green and blue; blue and red.

Although each chip bears two different colors, some of the chips are duplicated, thus they form a sizable group.

The performer explains that he wants someone to stack the chips, picking any that he desires, but always placing spots of the same color together. For example: Suppose the person picks up a chip that has red on one side, orange on the other. If he holds it with the red spot up, he must then find a chip with a red spot and set its red side downward upon the first chip.

Assuming that a blue spot shows on top of this second chip, the person must pick another chip that has a blue spot, which is accordingly set upon the blue spot that already shows, making blue meet blue.

19

---

[5]Remember I said before that palming is when you secretly hold something in your hand without the audience realizing it.

At any time the whole stack may be turned over, to use the color which appears upon the bottom of the stack. Sometimes this is necessary, as the person stacking the chips may run out of those that have a spot with the required color to continue stacking upward.

The object is to use up the entire stack of chips, totaling more than a dozen, by stacking them in this haphazard fashion. Should the person find the process blocked by any mistake or wrong calculation, he must begin again.

Once all the chips are stacked, persons are told to note the color of the spot that tops the stack; also the color of the spot on the bottom. They concentrate on those colors and after a few moment, the performer names them: for instance, Blue and Red.

Method: There are fifteen chips in the set, three each of the following combinations: Red-Orange; Orange-Yellow; Yellow-Green; Green-Blue; Blue-Red. But in giving out the chips, the performer retains one so the person who does the stacking is only using fourteen.

The performer turns away during the stacking process. This gives him a chance to observe the colors of the spots on the chip he has retained, for example, Blue-Red. When the stack is complete and he is asked to name the top and bottom colors, he names Blue and Red. No matter how the stack has been gathered, those colors will be correct.

To repeat the trick, the performer gathers the chips, adding the one he already has. Secretly retaining another chip, he notes its colors to learn the top and bottom spots of the next stack.

This trick can easily be made by using a package of white poker chips. Put an Avery 3/4" dot on each side of the chips as described. This trick is also commercially available under the title of "Spots Before Your Eyes."

8. Sometimes My Pen Gets Shrinkage

Effect: The magician holds a pen in his hands and as he passes the pen from hand to hand the pen appears to shrink until it's about half of it's original size.

Method: This illusion is quite similar to that old trick where you make a pencil seem like it's made of rubber by holding it at its center and shaking it up and down. To make a pen shrink you simply have to pass the pen from hand to hand holding it horizontally between the fingers and the thumb . The faster you pass the pen the smaller it will seem to appear.

It is a visual illusion that is guaranteed to work. Often as you perform magic somebody might ask you to do a trick on the spot. This is perfect improvisational effect. I find that spectators often ask the question, "How do you do it?" They also ask me if I could teach them a trick. I find this is an ideal trick to teach them to get them in order to stop nagging me. This is the perfect effect to teach someone because there is nothing to teach. What you see is what you get. In the end, everyone leaves happy – I because the audience member has stopped nagging me and I didn't have to give away any of my secrets, and the audience member because they learned a cool little trick to impress their family, friends, and foes with .

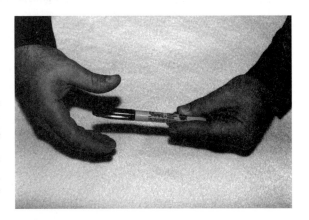

9. Bottle and Pills

21

Effect: This baffler has the elements of an escape mystery, reduced to pocket proportions. The performer introduces a pill bottle of cylindrical shape and a few pellets which he terms pills. These pills are of a sort that will not dissolve in water as the performer demonstrates by dropping them in the bottle, filling it with water and then corking it.

Now, placing the bottle under a handkerchief, the performer produces a very puzzling result. After manipulating it a few moments, he brings out the bottle in one hand, the pills in the other. The bottle is still corked and filled with water, which raises the query: How could it be done? People who want to try it are baffled before they begin. They just can't take the pills from the bottle without pouring out the water first. Nevertheless, the impromptu wizard did it!

Method: Here's how: The pills are actually metal pellets, painted white. Instead of pills, sequins or beads may be used, but in any case they must be metal, and of a magnetic type. The wizard also uses a tiny but powerful magnet. With his hands beneath the handkerchief, which he keeps draped over them, the magician uncorks the bottle, places the magnet at the outside near the bottom and moves it up to the top.

Magnetized through the glass, the pills come along. Once they are out of the top of the bottle the cork is replaced. The magnet can be attached to a finger ring, but in this particular trick it is better to have it concealed in the cork. It should be in the top half of the cork, so as not to attract the pills while they are first exhibited in the bottle. When the cork is removed from the bottle under the handkerchief, it is used as the magnet, then replaced.

Instead of placing the magnet inside a cork it would be easier to simply glue a magnet inside the top of a pill bottle. After affixing the magnet to the top of the cover of the pill bottle, paint the magnet to match the cover.

10. Magnetized Glasses

Effect: Using a book about the size of this volume, also a pair of small, light drinking glasses, the magician proceeds to demonstrate a feat of actual Oriental wizardry. This trick was originally used as a close-up mystery by wonder workers in the Far East.

A handkerchief is wrapped around the book and the magician inverts the glasses upon it, side by side, a space of about an inch between them. Pressing his first two fingers between the glasses, he slides his thumb under the book, then turns it over, handkerchief and glasses with it. Amazingly, the glasses remain suspended from what is now the bottom of the book.

Afterward, glasses and book are given for examination, to show that they could not have been attached in any manner, though the presence of the intervening handkerchief was in itself a proof that trickery was absent.

Method: Actually, the trick is in the handkerchief, the only item that seems completely free of suspicion. Two round beads are tied together with less than an inch of cord between them. The hem of a handkerchief is opened and the beads are put inside it. In wrapping the prepared handkerchief around the book, the magician can feel the beads and arrange them so that they are side by side, fairly near the edge of the book.

The glasses are inverted side by side, each so its rim is over a bead. As they are slid apart, the rims engage the hidden beads. The fingers are pressed between to exert outward pressure, thus holding the glasses in place when the book is turned upside down.

11. Three Divining Rods

Effect: Showing three small wooden cylinders, each about two inches in length and the thickness of a pencil, the magician states that they are divining rods. Each is painted a different color, as red, green, and blue. Their peculiarity, according to the magician, is that their colors can be distinguished even when they are out of sight.

To prove this, the magician supplies a metal tube with a cap that fits over it. There is a small hole in the bottom of the tube, so that when one of the wooden divining rods is inserted, the air will emerge when the rod is pushed down, as it is a fairly tight fit. The ends of all the rods are painted black, so that it would be impossible to tell them apart by looking through the hole.

While the magician's back is turned a rod is placed in the tube and the tube covered with the cap. Then it is dropped in the magician's hand behind his back.

The other two rods are kept from sight while the magician concentrates on the color of the rod in the tube and soon names it correctly. The tube, is returned to the spectators, rod and all, and the trick may then be repeated.

Method: The hole in the tube is more important than supposed. The rods have corresponding holes in both ends, but they are scarcely noticeable, as they are smaller and painted black. Behind his back, the magician takes a pin which is fastened under his coat and presses it up through the hole in the tube into the rod.

The depth to which the pin goes tells the color, as the holes in the rod are drilled accordingly. Just past the pin point indicates the red rod. About half the pin's length means green. If the pin goes nearly all the way, the rod in the tube is blue.

23

Part 2
Card Tricks

Essentially every card trick works the same way. The formula is as follows: spectator chooses card + magician finds chosen card = card trick. In performance the formula may sound like this "Hi, my name is Nick and I've got a trick that will certainly make your mind tick. Pick a card. Any card (Yeah right!). Remember your card. Now place it anywhere in the deck (Even though I'm having you place the card exactly where I want you to place it)." Then the magician sets the entire deck on fire which burns in a flash, except for one card. And wouldn't you know that the one card to survive is the chosen card[1].

Although this is a simple formula, there are thousands of variations. There are hundreds of ways to achieve these variations. You can have the chosen card appear on a palm pilot. Perhaps the chosen card will vanish from the deck and appear in your pocket. Or even better, in a spectator's pocket. What if the card vanished and appeared two weeks later in the spectator's pants pocket and the pants weren't even the same pants that the spectator wore when they saw the trick. Now, perhaps, you can see how magicians come up with thousands of variations on the same card formula. In this chapter I plan to teach you the basics that will allow you to be creative and create your own variations on this very simple formula.

There are two exceptions to this formula. The first is that you will predict what card is chosen. For example: The magician writes the name of a card on a piece of paper, puts the paper in an envelope, seals the envelope, and gives it to a third party to guard. Then the spectator chooses a card. The magician has the third party open the envelope and show that the card name written on the paper is the same as the chosen card.[2]

The second type of card trick combines another magic principle with the card effect. One example of this is combining the magic principle of restoration with a card trick. The result might be where a magician has a spectator choose a card. The magician then rips the card into pieces. He tucks the pieces into his

---

[1] This trick will be explained later in the chapter.

[2] Also explained later in the chapter

25

fist and says the magic word, "flumadiddle." When the magician opens his fist, the spectator's card has been restored to one piece. Or perhaps the magician combines the principle of levitation and the card floats out of the deck and into the magician's hands.

This chapter is split up into five sections:

Section 1 - Card Sleights
Section 2 - Using the sleights
Section 3 - Tricks for people who don't want to practice sleights but want to look like they've got the best hands in the business.
Section 4 - Tricks that will impress everyone but mathematicians
Section 5 - Trick decks (that can be used to drive the mathematicians crazy).

Section 1: Card Sleights

I was once at a magic convention when I heard some guy say this, "Hey, you want to see my triple lift one handed false cut bottom deal riffle spinner, which when caught properly, sets me up for the un-dominant handed elmsely count? It took me three months to learn and eight months to master." My point is that the magic jargon is overwhelming, but a few key basic words will take you a long way. For this chapter you need to be familiar with the following terms: **key card, force,** and **Control**.

Key Card - any card that acts as a marker to tell you where the selected card is.
Force - forcing the spectator to pick a particular card while making them believe that they have the freedom to choose any of the 52 cards that they want.
Control - controlling the selected card to the top or bottom of the deck without the spectator realizing it.

1. Using the Key Card
The key card allows for the magician to find the location of the chosen card in the deck without knowing what the chosen card is. The key card is placed on the bottom of the deck. Lets say we choose the Ace of Hearts as the key card. After the

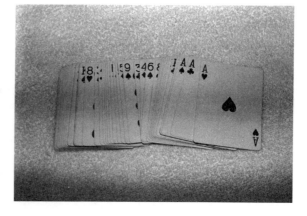

spectator pulls a card out of the deck, cut the top half of cards off the deck and have the spectator place their card on top of this pile. For the sake of greater clarity in this explanation I have marked the spectator's card with the name Matt on the back Then place the bottom half on top of the spectators card. To the spectator it will seem as if the card was placed somewhere in the middle of the deck. What the

spectator does not realize is that a key card is directly on top of the chosen card. This enables the magician to quickly search through the deck and find the key card, and in turn find the chosen card which is right beside it.

Helpful Hints

· The key card can always be what ever card is on the bottom of the deck at the time. A terrific method for sneaking a peak at the bottom card is to ask a spectator to shuffle the cards. The bottom card can almost always be seen during a riffle shuffle[3]. Allowing

the spectator to riffle shuffle the cards has the added benefit of making the magician seem less suspicious.

·When having the person place the card back into the deck you can riffle[4] through the cards and ask them to say stop. Wherever they say stop is where

[3.] Riffle Shuffle - a shuffle done by splitting the deck into two piles, on in each hand. The thumbs pull the two piles up and drop the cards down one at a time over each other.

[4.] Riffle - to thumb through the deck so that each card falls down one at a time.

27

you cut the deck. By asking them to say stop, you are making them believe that they are choosing where the card goes; which has a two fold purpose. First it gives the spectator a choice which makes them feel less suspicious, and second it takes the attention away from the point that you are cutting the bottom portion of the deck over the top.

2. Forcing a Card: "Use the force Luke, Use the Force"

If it's good enough for Yoda, it's good enough for me. The card force is a thing of sheer beauty. Once you have forced a card upon a spectator, you have opened up the doorway to an infinite amount of possibilities in which you can find the chosen card. I will show you three different forces: **The Hindu Shuffle force, The cut force, and the bottom card slide force.** I recommend that you learn and try all three and eventually let one naturally become your dominant force.

The Cut Force:
This is the easiest force in the mechanical sense, but the most difficult force in the acting sense. Place the card you want forced (lets say it's the Ace of Hearts which

28

is marked by a white "X" on the back) on the top of the deck. Have a spectator cut the deck in half. Then place the bottom half of the deck on top of the top half. When you complete this cut give the top half a 90 degree twist. Here comes the misdirection part. This is where I said that it might get difficult in the acting sense. The challenge is to misdirect the spectator's atten-tion away from the cards. Talk a

little. Pretend you forgot the instructions to the trick and take out a little cheat cheat and pretend to quickly read it. After your few moments to get the spectator's direction away from the cards, have them lift up the top pile and look at the card underneath (which is the forced card).

The Hindu Shuffle Force:

1. Place the card you want to force (lets say the Ace of Hearts) on the bottom of the deck.

2. Hold the pack of cards in your left hand. Make sure the pack is face down.

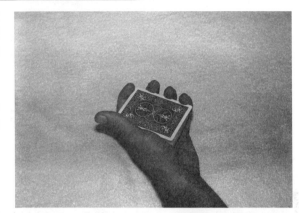

3. Pick up a good chunk of the pack, maybe 2/3rds, with your right hand. It is important to leave the bottom 1/3rd of the pack in your hand because you do not want to shuffle your force card into the deck.

29

4. Bring your right hand, holding the top portion of the deck over your left hand. Touch the two top corners together. Grab a small chunk of cards (4-6 cards at a time) off the pile in the right hand with the fingers and thumb from the left hand.

5. Pull the right hand away while the left fingertips and thumb hold the chunk of cards.

When the right hand is cleared away, drop the cards in the left fingertips and thumb on top of the pile in the left hand.

6. Repeat steps 4-5 until you've transferred all the cards from the right hand to the left. Note that your forced card will still be on the bottom. As you are doing steps one three six say, "As I'm shuffling the cards like this, I would like for you to just say stop." By the time you finish the sentence you should also be completing step six. Make sure that the spectator understands your instructions.

7. Start the hindu shuffle again, except this time grab the entire pack with the right hand and start steps 4-5. Now the bottom card in the pack that is held in the right hand is the forced card. Keep shuffling until the spectator says stop, which will usually occur at some point when approximately half the deck has already been removed. After the spectator says stop, show the spectator the bottom card (forced card) in the pack held by the right hand. The effect, to the spectator, will be that you showed them a card that was somewhere in the middle of the deck. Hold the card up for a brief pause and say "Memorize this card. Do you have it memorized?" When they say "yes," slap the top portion of the deck that is in the right hand over the bottom. At this point the card is forced and you are free to milk out the rest of the magic trick.

Helpful Hints

•After they say stop during the hindu shuffle, you may ask "Are you sure? You can change your mind." This is a subtle way of saying "pick a card, any card." It reinforces the idea in the spectators mind that they really have the freedom to choose any card.

·If you have shuffled off most of the cards from the pack in the right hand and the spectator still hasn't said stop, take the cards from the right pack and place them on the table(thus keeping the forced card still on the bottom) then grab half of the cards from the pack in the left hand and place them on top of the pack that's on the table.Then grab the remainder of the cards in the left hand with the right hand and place those on the pack. Tell the spectator, "You understand that you're supposed to say stop while I'm shuffling, right?" Then start the hindu shuffle all over again.

Bottom Card Slide Force

The bottom card slide force was the first force I ever learned. It's simplistic nature makes it all the more powerful. Start by placing the forced card (let's say the Ace of hearts) on the bottom of the deck.

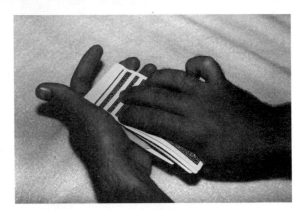

1. Hold the pack in the left hand using the thumb and finger tips.
2. Place right thumb under the pack sandwiched between the left hand and deck of cards. This setup keeps the thumb on the forced card.
3. The fingers of the right hand should start collecting the cards. The right middle finger should touch every card as it sweeps it into the right hand. Ask an audience member to say stop on any card. The effect is that you will show them any card they choose.
4. After the spectator has said

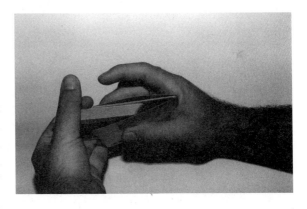

31

stop, the right hand should pull away from the left hand grabbing the chosen card with the rest of the cards above it. Simultaneously, the thumb is pulling the bottom card (the forced card) from the pack. Lift the pack in the right hand to show the spectator the card they think they chose and after a brief pause drop the pack back on top of the cards in the left hand. Your force is complete and you are free to milk out the remainder of the effect.

3. Controlling A Card

The beauty of controlling a card is that you can tell your audience that you are controlling the card and they will still be impressed. Sometimes the fact that your mastery of sleight of hand is so immense, is impressive in and of itself.

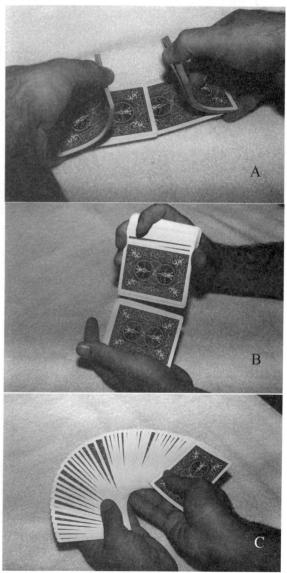

A

B

C

32

The Over Hand Shuffle:
The overhand shuffle is a common shuffle used by people who don't know how to or do not have the dexterity to do a riffle shuffle.**(Pic A)**. The cards are held horizontally in the right hand while the left thumb sweeps the top few cards into the left hand. The right hand moves up and down over the left hand, each time dropping off a few more cards.**(Pic B)**. This false shuffle has been chosen for three reasons: (1) It is a natural shuffle that many people do or have seen done before thus making it less

suspicious; (2) Because many people are familiar with or can already do this shuffle it will be easier to learn; and (3) it's a natural shuffle, and natural movements in magic can't be stressed enough.

1. Have a person choose a card. This is most commonly done by fanning the cards. **(Pic C)**

2. Begin to do your over hand shuffle and ask the spectator to say stop. Try to time your shuffle so that a quarter of the deck is in the left hand when they say stop. Have the spectator place their card on top of the pile in the left hand. The spectator's card has been marked with an "X" on the back. Make sure to square-up the pile that is in the left hand.

3. The pile in the left hand should be squared-up with the chosen card now on top. Three fingers should be holding the cards while the index finger is on the side. This set-up is important for the sleight to work.

33

4. Now here comes the first secret move. When the right hand brings the pile down to the left to drop more cards off, have the cards fall so that they are about a quarter of an inch in front of the pile already in the left hand. This creates an out-jog. The cards from the right hand should slightly cover the index finger of the left hand.

5. Then continue the remainder of the shuffle as you normally would. When you are dropping the last pile of cards from the right hand you pick up the original pile made before the out-jog with the right hand and then drop it on the remainder of the cards in the left hand. This controls the chosen card to the top of the deck.

The key to making the overhand shuffle control work is to practice making the movements as smooth and natural as possible. This control should look the same as when you are actually doing an overhand shuffle. A good way to practice this is to do a real overhand shuffle and then compare how it looks with the false overhand shuffle.

34

Section 2: Using the Card Sleights

Now that you understand how to find a chosen card using the key card, force a card, and control a card to the top of the deck, you have the tools to perform hundreds of card tricks. It's sort of like learning three chords on the guitar and then being able to play hundreds of rock n' roll songs. In this section, I will show you how some of these card sleights can be used to create astonishing effects. I also encourage you to be creative and try to discover ways of incorporating these sleights into your own routines and original effects..

Name that Card

Effect: The cards are shuffled by a spectator. The magician instructs the spectator to fan the cards face down across a table. The magician asks the spectator to choose a card by pulling it out of the fan without looking at it. The spectator writes their name on the back of the card. The card is than placed in the middle of the deck. Neither the magician or the spectator knows what the card is. The spectator than fans the cards face up. The magician has the spectator find the card using his intuition. As the magician runs his fingers across the fanned deck of cards the spectator tells him to stop. Let's suppose the magician stops over the three of clubs. The card is pulled out and turned over to find that it was the chosen card that the spectator had signed.

Method: The beautiful part about this effect is that the magician gives the spectator credit for doing the trick. The magician never even has to touch the cards. This effect is accomplished by a method known as the key card.

1. The magician gives the cards to a spectator to shuffle. Ask if there is anyone who knows how to riffle shuffle and then give them the cards. As they shuffle take a peak at the bottom card (which is naturally spotted during this type of shuffle). If the bottom card is the ace of hearts than that becomes your key card.

2. Now have the spectator fan the cards face down across the table and pull out a card without looking at the face. While the spectator is signing their name on the back of the card, have another spectator collect the cards. The key card should still be on the bottom.

3. Then have the cards cut just the same way as explained in how to use the key card. When the cut is completed the ace of hearts should be right next to the chosen card.

4. Have the cards fanned across the table again, except this time they should be face up. Look for the card just above the key card to find the chosen card.. From here on the rest of the trick is acting.

5. Run your fingers across the cards and when ever the spectator says stop, eliminate the cards away from the key cards. Then run you finger across in the opposite direction and continue to eliminate cards until you are

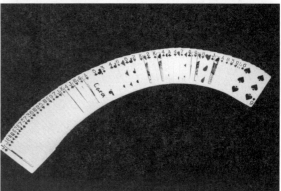

left with two cards, the chosen card and either of the adjacent cards.

6. At this point say to the spectator, "Please point to one of these cards." If the spectator points to the chosen card, eliminate the other card and say "so this is that card that you chose. Now please turn it over. Is that your signature?" If the spectator points to the non-chosen card then simple take that card away and say, "so you've eliminated this card with the rest of them. So we are finally left with this one card. Please turn it over. Is that your signature?"

At this point accept the thunder like applause that typically follows. The nice part about this trick is that the spectator gets to go home with their signed card as a souvenir. The less than nice part about this trick is that you lose a card and can only perform it about 15 times until you have to get a new deck of cards. This is a good opener card trick because it gets the audience in the magic mood. Especially if you explain to them that much of how a magician performs their magic is through toning their skills of intuition. Then tell them that they also have intuition skills and begin the trick. The success of this lies in that you do not try to make it too outrageous. The truth is that most people want to believe that they could develop their skills of intuition so are willing to go along with this little fib that you provide them with.

Look What Popped Up!

Effect: This effect always brings excitement to the audience with its surprising climax. A spectator chooses a card and then places it back into the deck. The magician shuffles the deck of cards and then holds it approximately a foot over the table. The deck is dropped on to the table and the impact of the cards hitting the table causes the chosen card to jump to the top the pack and flip itself over.

Method: The powerful effect is easily accomplished by controlling the chosen card to the top of the deck. Use the overhand shuffle to accomplish this. Once the card is on top of the pack the hard part is over and the rest of the trick is a breeze. Hold the deck with the right hand and use the left thumb to push the top card over a bit. Drop the pack from about a foot over the table and upon landing the top card will flip itself over.

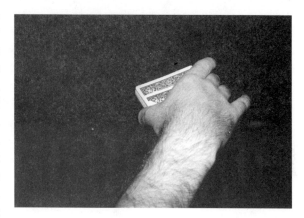

37

Card on Wall

I remember when I first got to Gainesville and people found out that I was a magician. They all said to me, "Have you seen Magic Mike yet? He's the guy who works at restaurants and throws cards on the ceiling." He became legendary for performing this card trick.

Effect: A card is chosen and shuffled back into the deck. The magician then takes the deck and throws it against a wall where all the cards fall except for the chosen card. The chosen card reveals itself stuck to the wall.

Method: Once again you must use the false overhand shuffle to control the chosen card back to the top of the deck. Then a piece of tape is secretly placed on the back of the chosen card. When the cards are thrown against the wall, the chosen card will stick while the other cards fall to the floor. The following two methods explain how to get the tape onto the card without the audience realizing it.

Method 1:

1. Prepare the tape by attaching it to itself to create a sticky loop. Then stick the loop to your pants by the right side pocket.

2. After controlling the selected card to the top of the deck with the false overhand shuffle, square up the cards and hold them in your left hand.
   Hold the cards up to a volunteers mouth and ask the volunteer to blow on the deck. This movement acts as misdirection because   simultaneously as the volunteer is blowing on the pack of cards, your right hand falls to the side pocket where you secretly swipe the piece of tape.

3. The Piece of tape should be wrapped around   A

the ring finger. By bringing the cards back and placing them in the right hand face-up, you automatically attach the tape to the back of the top card.

Simply remove your finger from the loop and you're all set. This is a sensitive part of the trick because you do not want the audience to notice that you are applying adhesive tape to the back of a card. Believe me, they'll be looking for a sneaky move. No pressure. The best way to reduce and exterminate audience suspicion during this time is to relax. If you're relaxed your audience will relax. Another way to get your audience to chill out is to make them laugh. After the volunteer has blown on the cards you could say something like, "I said blow, not spit." This may cause your volunteer to become

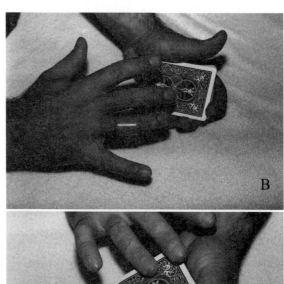

embarrassed but sometimes there are casualties in this art called magic. You could even take this a step further by pretending to be upset and say, "Great! Now you've made my cards sticky. I can't work with sticky cards!" Throw a temper tantrum, as well as the cards, and leave the room as if really upset. This reaction always leaves the audience puzzled; if not by the chosen card stuck to the wall, than by the sensitive temperament of the entertainer.

Method 2:
Start the trick with the loop of tape on your finger and perform the entire trick this way. Your casual behavior and movements will mask the tape. This method is much bolder but also more exciting; that is, if your into that sort of excitement. If you don't believe that it works, look back in the Introduction (where the five card prediction is in intro. Have tape on fingers holding cards). Did you notice the tape on my finger? If so, did you disregard it?

The Nested Card Boxes

Effect: The magician brings out a briefcase and tells the audience, "I had a premonition earlier today. I had the strongest feeling that a certain card would be chosen by a certain spectator. I envisioned a person with... (describe the features of a person in the audience). Would you please help me to see if my premonition was correct. In this briefcase I have placed a duplicate of the card that I think you are about to choose." The magician gives the briefcase to another member of the audience and tells them "watch this briefcase and make sure nobody tampers with it." The spectator chooses a card and shows it to the audience. Then the briefcase is opened and a sealed box is pulled out. The box is opened and another smaller box which has an envelope inside of it is opened. The sealed envelope is torn open to reveal a duplicate of the original card.

Method: You must prepare this trick by taking a card and placing it in a sealed envelope, which will be sealed in a box, which will be sealed in a larger box... which will be sealed inside of a briefcase. How many levels you use to seal the card is up to you. Just note that you don't want the volunteer to spend too much time opening up the boxes and envelopes looking for the card. Once the briefcase is prepared, you simply have to force a card on the spectator and the rest is acting. You can use any of the forces mentioned earlier for this trick. (Hindu shuffle, half-cut force, bottom card slide force.)

Card thru Curtain and window: Cousin to Card on Wall

Effect: The magician has a spectator choose a card and replace it back into the deck. The magician then tells the audience, "I'm going to throw these cards against the curtain and the spectator's card will stick to the curtain." The magician throws the pack of cards against the curtain but the chosen card does not remain stuck against the curtain. The magician pretends that something has gone wrong but suddenly realizes what happened. The magician says, "Oh, you know what might have happened? I think I may have thrown the cards a bit too hard." A spectator pulls the curtain away only to find the selected card stuck to the other side of the window. The magician acts surprised and says, "Wow, it appears that the card went through the curtain and the glass.

Method: This trick is quite similar to the card on the wall in appearance but completely different in methodology.

1. Prepare the trick by sticking a duplicate of the forced card (with either adhesive tape or rubber cement) to the window.
2. Make sure to force the same card that you stuck to the window. The trick just isn't as impressive when the wrong card appears on the window. You may use any of the forces discussed earlier (Cut Force, Hindu Shuffle Force, Bottom Card Slide Force).
3. Once you've forced the card the rest of the trick is acting. Build up the story about how it's going to stick to the curtain - it will make the moment funnier when nothing stays there. Act sincere about not knowing what happened to the card. It will build suspense. Finally, have one of the spectators pull away the curtain and find the card so that there is no way you can be accused of quickly planting it there. Sometimes I'm accused of doing things that, if I had done them, would be more impressive than the actual trick.

Tips:

41

•Make sure to plant the card way in advance before you perform the trick. Sometimes when I'm hired to perform close-up magic at a party I get the urge to sneak into their house the night before and plant cards all over the place. Of course, I've never acted on this urge. Really, I haven't.
•Do the trick when you are already by the curtain and window to avoid the suspicion of taking a group across the house past three or four windows to the exact window that you want.

•Another idea here is to use an accomplice. Ask a friend who has already seen you perform this trick to go plant a card on the window. Then when your mingling with a group of people by that window have the friend come up to the group and say, "Hey can you show us that card on the wall trick I saw you do last weekend?" Then everyone will start to coax you into performing. At this point, if your brave, you could bluff and say, "I really didn't prepare anything for tonight." The audience will just be more adamant about seeing you perform. Someone might even say, "Come-on, if you were a real magician you wouldn't have to prepare." You could even go as far as saying, "I didn't bring a deck of cards with me though." Then have your confederate say, "Wait, I've got a deck of cards. If you're a real magician you should be able to use my deck" Meanwhile he's giving you the deck of cards you asked him to hold on to when you also asked him to plant the card for you. But then again, you don't want to take your bluff too far because subtlety is the art of good bluffing. The nice thing about using a confederate is that you don't have to do the dirty work of planting the card. The rotten thing about using a confederate is that you have to let them in on the trick.

If you're worried about your audience noticing the chosen card on the floor after the cards are thrown against the curtain you have two options. One is to rubberband the pack before you throw it in order to keep the forced card secured somewhere in the middle of the deck. This is nice because you don't have to mess around with picking up the cards. But I like the second option better. Perform the trick the same way as card on the wall. Force the card, but then control the card to the top of the deck. Have a spectator blow on the cards and then make the joke: "I said blow, not spit." Then go on about how the cards are now too soggy and you can't perform the trick. Place the cards in your pocket and pretend to be done. Then say, "Just kidding." Pull the cards out of your pocket, leaving the top card (the forced card) in your pocket . Then continue the trick as before. I like the second method better for three reasons: (1) It involves more acting which is more fun for you

and the audience, (2) I think that it creates a better spectacle when the cards go flying everywhere, and (3) you are truly left clean at the end of the trick. If someone accuses you of using a duplicate card and wants to search through the cards on the floor, you can let them. You can also have them pick up the cards while they're down there. Actually, when I'm pretending that the trick has gone wrong I sometimes go as far as have the spectators look for the card. When the card can't be found, I then have a spectator discover it behind the window.

42

Having Fun with the Forces

In the spirit of planting cards places, you don't have to limit yourself to windows. You could plant a card anywhere; under a lamp, in the vase that sits on the mantel over the fireplace, under the phone, in a medicine cabinet, underneath the cushion of a couch, and the list could go on forever. Once I planted a card in my sister's home and did the card trick which revealed the planted card two weeks later. I encourage you to be creative and have fun with planting cards.

Another thing I like to do with a force is mindreading. I force a card, lets say the ace of hearts, then begin acting. I often take out a pad and pencil and scribble all over it as if that helps me to read the spectator's mind. Another thing that I do is draw out the mindreading process. After they pick a card I don't just say "ace of hearts, right?" No, I milk it for everything it's worth. I first start off my guessing the color of the suit. Then what suit it actually is. I'll ask the spectator to visualize that they are sending me the card. Get them real into it. Then I narrow it down to whether it's a face card or number card. I figure out if it's a high number. finally, when they can't take the suspense anymore, I tell them what card they are thinking of. Sometimes you'll get a wise-guy who will do anything to try to make you look stupid; even lie about the card that they chose. To avoid this I'll either have the person write down the card and tell them that this will help them to visualize the card, or I show the chosen card to everyone in the audience.

43

Final Note With Sleights:

I want to stress that these card sleights are valuable tools and their possibilities are only limited by your creativity. Once you have mastered these sleights, you have opened the door to hundreds of cards tricks. The card tricks that I explained using the key card, control, and force are a good way to learn and practice the sleights, but I challenge you to come up with original routines that fit your personality.

Section 3: Tricks For People Who Don't WantTo Practice Sleights But Want ToLook Like They've Got The Best Hands In The Business.

Fastest Hands in Magic

Effect: Magician tells the audience "My goal is to have the fastest hands in magic. In magic they test your dexterity and speed with how fast you can find a card." Then the magician fans out the deck and has a volunteer put two cards anywhere in the deck. The magician squares up the pack and tells his audience, "OK, watch carefully because I'm going to try to make this as fast as I can." The magician throws the pack from one hand to the next and in the process removes the two cards.

Method: The two cards that the magician shows the audience are imposters.
1. Prepare for this trick by pulling out the Queen of Diamonds and the Jack of Hearts. Place one of the cards on top of the deck and the other card on the bottom. Then pull out the Queen of Hearts and Jack of Diamonds and place those both on the top of the deck. Now your set to go.

44

2. Give your audience the spiel about having the fastest hands. Then show the audience the two cards, fan the deck, and ask a spectator to place them anywhere in the deck.

3. Now square up the pack and give the audience more spiel about how they should look real carefully because you're going to be so fast. Then hold the pack with your right hand, thumb on top and your fingers on the bottom.

4. Now throw the pack to your left hand but grip the top two cards with your right hand. The pack should easily slide between the two cards. This move takes a little bit of practice but is fairly simple. Show the two imposter cards and accept your applause.

The Four Jacks

A similar trick to the fastest hands in magic is the four Jacks. This is one of those card tricks that every magician learns when they are first introduced to magic.

Effect: The magician takes the four Jacks and places them on top of the deck. He then takes three of the four jacks and places them into different parts of the deck. He puts the deck on a table, passes his hands over the cards, and magically all four Jacks join together on the top of the deck.

45

Method: Your never actually put the four Jacks in the middle of the deck.

1. Prepare the trick by taking out the four jacks and three other cards. Square up the three random cards and place one of the jacks over it.

2. Place the other jacks fanned out on top of the first Jack. It should look as if you have only the four jacks fanned out.

3. Square up the pack of supposedly four jacks (but really seven cards) and put them on top of the deck. Then take the top three cards (none jacks) and place them in different parts of the deck.

4. Turn over the fourth card (one of the jacks) and say, "I'm going to leave the last Jack on top as a locator card." Then turn it face down again. Create a magical move (like tapping the deck three times, waiving your hands over the deck, snapping, or even wiggling your finger at the deck while saying a magic word like "flummadiddle") and perform it now. Then turn over

the top four cards to show your audience that all jacks are on the top of the deck. You may also give them the deck and your magic wiggling fingers to examine.

The Upside-Down Card

46

Effect: A card is chosen and replaced back into the deck. The magician then spreads the cards across a table and shows that the selected card has turned itself upside-down.

Method: Once nice thing about this effect is that it can be done with anyone's card and the preparation is simple.

1. Prepare for this trick by taking the bottom card in a deck and turning it face up.

2. Then Fan the cards out and have a spectator pick a card. Be sure not to show the face up bottom card when you do this.

3.   Here's where the secret move happens. Tell the spectator to show his card to the audience. While everyone is looking at the card, square up the pack and turn the entire deck over. Now only the top card should be face down while all the other cards are face up.

4.   Have the spectator slide their card in the middle of the deck. There should now only be two cards that are face down – the selected card and the top card.

5.   Explain to the audience that the card has already turned itself over. Simultaneously turn the entire pack over again. I know this seems daring but if your talking and looking into the people's eyes, they'll be looking into your eyes.   The subtle movement of turning the pack over will be undetectable to the audience, especially if you are relaxed when you're do it.

6.   Now you are probably wondering how to turn over the bottom card without anyone noticing. Now I don't mean to toot my own horn but I think this is just short of flat out brilliant. You simply pull the bottom card away from the deck as you fan the cards out face up across the table. The audience will see that one card is turned face down. You then use the bottom card to flip over the fan. Can you believe it's that simple? It is absolutely natural to use a card to flip over a fan and the movement of fanning out the cards distracts the spectators from noticing which way the card was facing. I know this sounds bold, and frankly – it is bold. But it works.

Helpful Hints:

If you're really self-conscious about doing some of those bold moves there is an other less exciting option. You can tell the audience that you will find the card behind your back and flip it over. Then while the pack is behind your back you can flip over the top card and bring out the deck to show that you found their card by flipping it over. I'm not as crazy about this method because it is less magical and people often try to peak behind your back.

    With either method it is important to fan the cards face up and let the audience see that one card is face down. This creates suspense which creates increased entertainment. Then flip over the fan to show all the cards face down except for the chosen one. This will accentuate the chosen card and act as a natural applause cue for your audience.

48

Section 4: Tricks that will impress everyone but mathematicians.

5. Three-Deal Prediction

Taking a shuffled pack of cards, the magician looks through the faces and states he will predict a card that a spectator will subconsciously select. The magician writes the name of the card on a slip of paper which is folded and placed aside for future reference.

    Spreading, the pack face down along the table, or running the cards from hand to hand, the magician tells the spectator to take three cards absolutely at random. Giving the pack to the spectator, the magician then instructs him to lay the three cards face up, side by side, and upon each card deal enough more to bring its total up to ten. The magician mentions that an Ace counts one, while any face cards stand for ten.

As example: Suppose the three cards are an Ace, a Seven, and a King. Upon the face-up Ace, the spectator deals nine cards from the pack; upon the Seven he deals three; upon the King, none.

That done, the spectator is told to add the values of the three cards he took. In the case mentioned, the Ace, Seven and King would count for one, seven and ten respectively, producing a total of eighteen. The spectator is told to count that many down in the pack and look at the final card-in this instance the eighteenth.

Suppose that card is the Four of Spades. When the spectator opens the folded paper, he finds the name "Four of Spades" written on it!

This trick works almost automatically. After a pack has been shuffled, the magician takes it and runs through the faces of the pack, secretly counting until he reaches twenty, from the face or bottom of the pack. This card, which will be the thirty-third from the top, is the one he predicts.

When the pack is spread face down, the magician merely sees to it that the three cards which the spectator takes are all above the thirty-third. This is easily handled by not spreading the bottom portion of the pack. Now, no matter what three cards the person takes, his deal and the count that follows Will bring him out on the thirty-third card.

Suppose the person takes three Aces. In dealing, he must bring their total up to ten, meaning thirty cards in all. Then he counts the values of the cards originally dealt: three Aces, totaling three. He counts that many from the pack and looks at the final card, which is therefore thirty-three. If higher cards than Aces are dealt, the count in each case is correspondingly less. The count simply subtracts from the deal.

Make sure beforehand that a complete pack is used and that it contains no joker. If there is a joker, you must count twenty-one cards from the bottom to make the prediction, instead of twenty. Should the spectator take a card below the thirty-third when the pack is spread, take a deep one yourself, lay it face up and explain how you wish him to count. Then put that card back in the deck, nearer the top. Another system to avoid trouble is to give the person half the pack and let him take three cards from it, while you look through the other half to make a prediction. Replace his half on top of yours and proceed with the trick.

6. Color Sense

As a dealing trick, this forms a pattern from which a variety of effects have been developed. In the direct form given here, it would seem that the performer was able to distinguish red cards from black while a spectator is dealing them, face down.

The performer tells a spectator to shuffle a pack; then begin dealing cards, face down. After a while, the performer tells the spectator to stop dealing and retain the balance of the pack. Picking up the dealt cards, the performer says: "You dealt just four more reds than you now have blacks in your hand. We'll count them and see." Running through the dealt heap, face up, the magician weeds out the red cards and counts them, finding sixteen. The spectator goes through the cards he holds, face up and discovers to his surprise that he has just twelve black cards.

The system is simply this: Take a pack of cards and divide it into two equal heaps of twenty-six each. Spread the heaps face up and you will find that you have exactly as many black cards in one heap as red cards in the other. If one heap has fifteen blacks, the other will have fifteen reds. Conversely the first heap will have eleven reds and the second heap eleven blacks. Though this sounds puzzling, it is simply a natural fact. The numbers may vary, but heaps will always balance in terms of reds in one heap, blacks in the other.

The trick of "Color Sense" is merely an extension of that fact applied to unbalanced heaps. Move a card from one equal heap to the other, making the heaps twenty-seven and twenty-five respectively. You will then find one more black in the larger heap than there are reds in the smaller heap. There will also be one more red in the larger heap than there are blacks in the smaller. For each card moved to the larger heap, the ratio will increase by one card more.

All the magician does when the spectator deals is keep counting the cards. As the count nears twenty-six, the magician says for the spectator to deal several more cards and then stop. Suppose the spectator stops on thirty. Being four more than twenty-six, four will be the ratio. Picking up the larger heap, the performer asks the spectator's preference: red or black. If red is stated, the performer says: "You dealt four more reds than you have blacks." Should the spectator pick black, the performer words it: "You dealt me four more blacks than you have reds." Either way, the fact is proven when the heaps are weeded.

The trick can be done with less than a full pack, provided an even number of cards is used. For instance with thirty-four cards, the magician must remember that seventeen is the balance point and handle things accordingly. In this case, should the spectator deal twenty cards, he would be giving the performer three more blacks than reds; also three more reds than blacks.

This trick may be repeated, but it is more effective to follow it with other dealing systems given in this chapter.

7. Faces Up

Taking a pack of cards, the magician turns a batch face up and riffles them in among the others so that the pack becomes a mixture of face-up and face-down cards. The magician invites a spectator to shuffle the pack thoroughly so there will be no chance of guessing which cards are which way.

Receiving the much mixed pack from the spectator, the magician places it behind his back, if he is standing, or beneath the table if he is seated. He says that without looking at the cards, he will tell which are face up and which are face down.

Shortly, the magician brings out the pack in two heaps, one in each hand. He states that be has divided them so that each heap contains exactly the same number of face-up cards. The heaps are spread by two spectators; each weeds out the face-up cards. They come to exactly the same number-say eleven face-up cards in each heap.

The trick is based on the rule of "balanced" heaps. Half of the pack (twenty-six cards) is turned face up, at the start, though the exact number should never be mentioned. No matter how thoroughly shuffled the pack may be, the performer has only to put it out of sight and count off the top twenty-six cards.

The situation will then be this: Either heap will contain exactly as many face-up cards as the other heap has face-down. That is, if the right-hand heap has eleven cards face up, there will be eleven face down in the left-hand heap. But this trick doesn't stop there. It has an added feature.

Having separated the two heaps, the performer turns over the cards in his left hand, while it is still out of sight. By doing this with the left-hand heap, he literally transforms its face-down cards into face-ups. Then when he brings the heaps into sight and gives each to a different person, a count of the cards will prove that each heap contains the very same number of cards face up!

It is a good plan to do this trick with less than a full pack, though not too many less; for example, from about thirty-four to forty-two, always using an even number. There are two reasons: Not only is the secret deal more rapid, but the spectators are not anxious to guess the number of cards that were originally face up. That number is generally different after the trick than at the start and with a full pack, someone might suspect all was equal at the outset.

51

Too few cards are also likely to betray the secret, hence the value of using an even total in the high thirties or low forties. There is also a neat throw-off that can be used with a considerable quantity of cards. Before receiving the pack, the performer asks that it be cut until there are some facedown cards on top. Taking the pack, he slides these over slightly and notices how many there are, say the three top cards.

The pack out of sight, the performer counts off the top half and Rips over the lower half, in the left hand. Then from the right-hand group, he pushes the three top (facedown) cards onto the left. Thus though the face-ups are equal in each heap, the heaps themselves will prove unequal should anyone decide to count them afterward. This will puzzle people who think they have a clue to the riddle.

Section 5: Trick Decks

Before I started performing magic I thought that there was only one type of trick deck – the crooked marked deck. A marked deck is a deck of cards with an elaborate pattern on the back of each card that hides subtle differences in the pattern that allow for the magician to be able to know the face of the card. You can always tell when a magician is working with a marked deck because they have to stare at the card for at least one minute to try and remember and calculate the code that distinguishes the fifty two cards.

I couldn't believe the variety of trick decks that were out there when I first started performing magic. I was suddenly able to perform modern day miracles with ease using my trick decks. Of course I was just a young ignorant budding magi at the time and didn't think it was at all suspicious that I pulled out a different deck of cards for each card trick that I performed. I also didn't think that it was suspicious that the card case said "Magic Stripper Deck."

I tell you this little tale to accentuate the point that a trick deck is only successful when nobody knows it's a trick deck. A statement that seems obvious but often overlooked. Now as you get more involved in magic, and perhaps join a magic club, you may run into magicians who look down upon people who use gimmick decks. These same magicians will preach that true sleight-of-hand artist are the only worthy magicians. My response to these outrageous claims is that the audience sees the effect not how the effect is accomplished. Remember that magic is about putting the wonder into people's heads not about how many cards you can palm.

I was once sitting at a lecture on cards at a magic convention and the lecturer started by having someone choose a card and then he read the mind of the spectator and revealed the chosen card. Now I want you to know that he was performing this for a group of magicians and he had all these magicians baffled. They all wanted to learn what kind of new force the lecturer had used. Then the lecturer told them that he had used a trick deck and the entire audience started to laugh because they realized they had been duped. They knew the magician was one of the world's best sleight-of-hand artist and they didn't suspect that he would use a trick deck. He further eliminated their suspicion by using a deck that was an exact replica of a regular bicycle deck of cards.

So if you are going to use a trick deck make sure that it looks legit. Magic shops often sell two types of decks, the ones that look fake and the ones that look real. It is worth the extra money to buy a legitimate looking deck. I tell you this based on the experience of having first gone through the fake looking decks.

There are reason why many close-up magicians stay away from trick decks though. Most close-up magicians work in restaurants and have to travel from table to table. For them, the less they have to carry the better off they are. Most often they would rather use a regular deck and not have to worry about carrying three or four decks. Many also want to hand out the cards and let the audience shuffle and inspect the decks. Although there are drawback to using a gimmick deck, the advantages can make them worth your while.

53

Svengali Deck

This is a forcing deck which means it allows for the magician to easily force a card on a person. In this deck every other card is the forced card (let's say the ace of hearts). The forced card is slightly shorter than the other cards which allows for the forced card to be forced when the cards are rifled and a spectator says stop. The deck can than be rifled to show that all the cards are the same as the forced card and then they can be riffled again to show that all the cards are different.

One of the big advantages to using a svengali deck is that you are unlimited by the amount of card tricks you can do. I suggest buying a book like *75 Tricks with a Svengali Deck* because it will give you many ideas for how to get the full use out of your deck. One draw back to the svengali deck is that you can only do one routine for an audience with that particular deck because it is meant to force only one card. I know that people often buy two or three svengali decks so that they can force different cards on people thus eliminating that suspicion.

Stripper Deck

The stripper deck is a controlling deck which means that it can control the chosen card or cards to either the top or bottom of the deck. The magician can even pull a chosen card right from the center of the deck. The way this deck works is that one of the sides of the pack is shaved down in an angle so that when a card is replaced back into the deck with a 180 degree turn, the edge sticks out. The edge that sticks out cannot be noticed by the audience but can easily be felt by the magician's fingers.

Like the svengali deck, there are numerous effects that can be done with the stripper deck. One of the advantages the stripper deck has over the svengali deck is that a multiple amount of cards can be used in one trick and different tricks can be done without having to switch decks. Again I recommend buying a book with this deck so that you can fully take advantage of the stripper deck's capabilities.

54

Rough/Smooth Decks

The rough/smooth is a principle that allows for two cards to stick together but can also be easily seperated. It allows for a deck to be fanned and only half the cards to be seen. A roughing spray is sprayed on to two cards and they are able to stick together, but they are also easily separated.

This principle is most famous in the trick known as *The Invisible Deck*. In this effect the magician asks the spectator to call out any card and then the magician pulls a pack of cards out of the case to show that the chosen card is the one card that is turned backwards in the pack. The even numbered cards are stuck to the odd numbered cards so that they are back to back. Depending on wether or not the chosen card is odd or even the magician pulls out the pack accordingly. The two cards that are stuck back to back should always add up to thirteen and hearts go with spades and diamonds go with clubs. For example if someone were to choose the eight of hearts it would be paired with the five of spades. So when the magician fingers through the pack and finds the paired card he simply separates it from the chosen card to show the chosen card turned upside down.

There are many effects that can be accomplished with rough/smooth decks. You can either buy the pre-made decks (like the invisible decks) or by roughing spray and make the trick decks yourself. Although it is cost effective to buy the roughing spray, most prefer to buy the decks because of how much time it takes to prepare the cards. If you do buy the roughing spray I recommend purchasing a book that will inform you as to how it can be used to its maximum capabilities.

55

Part 3
Stage Magic

The exigencies of present-day magic have been met by the development of many tricks which can be carried in small space, set up rapidly, and presented under almost any circumstances. Most of these are tricks requiring special apparatus of the sort to be described.

Formerly, small apparatus was used chiefly in platform shows, wherein the magician had something of the benefit of a stage, insofar as arranging his setting and allowing for angles of vision were concerned. Now, the magician may be called upon to perform at a banquet table or in the center of a nightclub floor, which means that he must meet problems for which much of the old-style apparatus was not designed.

Furthermore, many magicians now specialize in short acts, often giving more than one performance in an evening. They must get their tricks ready promptly and pack them up rapidly after finishing the act. Hence a suitcase show is adaptable to a variety of conditions and constitutes the stock-in-trade of many progressive performers.

Stage Magic is my favorite type of magic to perform. I like the grand aspect of performing to masses combined with the personal experience of close-up when I volunteer is brought on to the stage. This chapter is combined into two sections: (1) Effects that you can make, and (2) Effects that can be purchased. I prefer to build most of my props because I can cater them to my specifications and am completely aware of their capabilities. But there are effects that are simply easier to purchase and impossible to make on your own. When learning magic, I wish I had read a book that distinguished between these two sections so that I knew which tricks I didn't have to spend a fortune on because I could make them myself and which tricks I should invest in when shopping for something new at the magic shop.

Stage Effects That Can Be Made In Your Own Home

1. The Dye Box (Cereal Box)

Effect: The magician pulls a blue silk from his pocket and sticks it into an empty cereal box. He reaches into his pocket and finds that the blue silk has, by some unexplainable magical forces traveled to his pocket. To make sure it is the same silk he open the cereal box from both ends and looks through it carefully but finds no silk. He grabs the blue silk and places it back into the box. No sooner than when the box is closed does the silk jump back into his pocket. Again the audience sees the magician put the silk back into the box and again the silk jumps into the pocket. This time the magician pulls three blue silks out of his pocket, but instead of putting them into the cereal box, he shoves them back into his pocket. Then the magician shows the cereal box empty, closes it, gives it three shakes, and pulls the three blue silks out of it.

Method: This effect that I just explained is only one of many effects that can be performed with the die box. The die box is a utility item used for productions and disappearances. It is very similar to a change bag[1] except that it is much less expensive and fairly easy to make. There is a secret pocket in the dye box that is undetected by the audience in which small objects may be placed and seem to disappear.

Before explaining the routine I must explain how to construct a die box. I make mine out of two identical cereal boxes:

1. Carefully completely open one of the cereal boxes. Most cereal boxes are glued together on one of the thin sides. The box should be cut open, being sure not to tear any of the sides, so that it lays completely flat.

Lets call this first cereal box –Box A..

Box A

58

[1]Change Bag - A utility device in which objects such as silks can appear and disappear. This bag has a secret pocket that is unseen by the audience.

2. From box A cut off one of the large sides so that you are left with a large side and two thin sides . Also cut off the flaps from the thin sides.

3. Then from the box that has not been touched yet (we'll call this box B), carefully open the top and bottom of the box. Cut off the top flap that matches with the top tab from the other box .

Box A

Box A   Box B

59

Box A

4. Fold the side and bottom flap in on box A. Tape the bottom flap to the side flaps. Then place tape on all three flaps and stick the box A to box B so that the two front sides match up .

Now that your dye box is prepared you can begin your routine. You'll notice that if you look into your box from the bottom end the box looks

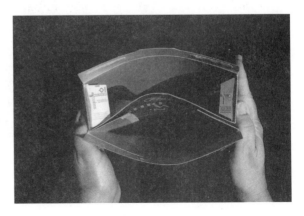

empty but if you look into the box from the top you can see that there is a secret pocket.

In order to perform the routine mentioned above, start by placing six blue silks into your pocket. Show the dye box from the bottom so that your audience can see that it is empty. Then close it. Take a silk from your pocket and place it into the cereal box, although you are really placing it into that secret pocket. Then here comes the acting part. Do some crazy wild gesture that makes the audience believe that the silk has jumped back into your pocket. Pull out a second blue silk from your pocket and then show the box is empty (again, this is accomplished by showing the box from the bottom so that the audience can see through it).

Take the silk and put it back into the box. You are actually loading the second silk into that secret pocket. Then do the whole crazy acting bit again showing that the silk jumped back into your pocket. Do the entire shtick again to load the third silk.

This time when your reach into your pocket pull out the last three silks and look frustrated. The audience may or may not laugh depending on how frustrated you look. Then get the idea to shove all three silks back into your pocket. Show the cereal box empty (again showing it from the bottom), close it up, give it a shake, and then pull all three silks from the box. Leave the three silks in the box and take your bow.

I want to reiterate that the die box is a magic utility device. There are many effects that can be performed with the dye box other than the one I described. You might even be able to find a book in your local magic shop called something like *50 Tricks with the Dye Box*. Understanding that the dye box is simply a tool to make things appear and disappear allows for an endless amount of possibilities for ways it can be performed. I highly recommend you create your own routine for this effect.

2. The Vanishing Coffee Cup

Effect: The magician displays a coffee cup on a saucer. He then takes a napkin and places it over the coffee cup. The magician lifts the coffee cup under the napkin off the saucer and throws it up in the air. The napkin slowly floats down showing that the coffee cup has vanished in mid air.

Method: The secret to this effect lies in the fact that the saucer, coffee cup, and napkin are all gimmicked.   Start by gluing a coffee cup to a saucer.   I strongly suggest you go to a dollar store and get a cheap coffee cup and saucer and not use any of the nice dishware or fine china in your home. Sorry Mom. Then cut a circle with the same circumference as the top of the coffee cup out of a piece of cardboard. Glue this between two paper napkins.

Now you are ready to begin the effect. Hold the saucer with the coffee cup on it in your left hand and use your right hand to place the napkin over the coffee cup and saucer. Line up the circular piece of cardboard with the top of the coffee cup. Tilt the saucer back so that the bottom of the faces the audience and the coffee cup faces your body. Simultaneously your right hand lifts the napkin at the edges of the cardboard creating the illusion that you are lifting the coffee cup from the rim. The coffee cup stays hidden behind the saucer. Drop the saucer off somewhere so that nobody can see it.   The rest is acting. You can throw the napkin up in the air or crumple it between your fingers. Either way you prove that the coffee cup has vanished.

Tips:

·The enlightening Gary Lightinheart came up with a method to do this effect in which the magician can show the coffee cup separate from the saucer. He glued magnets to the bottom of the coffee cup and metal washers to the saucer. This allowed him to show the two separate but also for the coffee cup to stick to the saucer, with the help of magnetic forces.

·I also recommend you perform this trick in context. What do I mean by that? I mean don't just say, watch me make this coffee cup disappear and poof it's gone. I recommend creating the gimmicked coffee cup and saucer out of an exact replica of the coffee cup in the local restaurant that you and your family or friend most frequently visit. I've often had waiters give me saucers and coffee cups after describing to them what I planned to do with it. Then wait and perform the effect at the restaurant. Now you're performing it in context and you are guaranteed to blow your friends into the land of dumbfoundem.

·Finally instead of gluing a piece of cardboard between two napkins you can sow it between two linen napkins. This simply makes the whole effect look classier. Again, if you're performing this in a restaurant use their napkins.

3. Cut & Restored String thru Straw

Effect: Magician threads a string through a straw. The magician then cuts the string and the straw in half. Yet when the magician pulls on one end of the string, the end from the cut half moves. And vice versa. Finally the magician pulls the entire string out of the straw to show that the string has been restored to one piece.

Method: The secret to this effect is in the straw. Before performing the trick, you must cut a one inch lengthwise slit into the center of the straw .**(Pic A)**. Then thread the string through the straw. Bend the straw in half, which opens the slit allowing for the string to drop through, and pull on the two ends of the string.**(Pic B)**. By pulling on the string ends, you are pulling the string down the slit. Now you can cut the straw without cutting the rope.

62

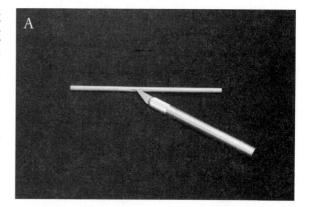

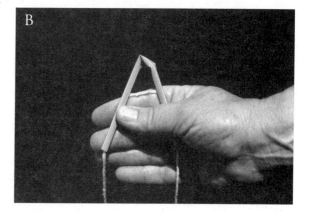

After cutting the straw in half, cross the top parts of the straw and use your fingers to cover the string. Now you can pull on either end of the string and the audience will be surprised as the opposite end rises. Finally pull the entire string out of the straw and show that it is completely restored.**(Pic C)**.

4. Bottle and Rope

Effect: The bottle used in this trick resembles an Oriental jar of squatty pattern with a narrow neck. Stating that the curious bottle has magnetic properties, the magician shows a length of rope which he claims is of the very sort used by Hindu rope climbers.

Dipping the rope into the bottle neck, the magician shows that it enters quite freely. But the rule of the Hindu Rope Trick is that what goes up does not come down. Therefore, in this case, what goes in will not come out. When the magician lifts the rope by the upper child, the bottle comes up with it, clinging mysteriously to the lower end of the rope.

The bottle may be swung back and forth on the rope end. Finally, still dangling from the rope, it is lowered into the hands of a spectator. Instantly the magnetism ceases. The rope comes free and the spectator is left with the bottle, which he may examine as much as he desires.

Method: This trick is an improvement on a "Rope and Vase" trick wherein the rope was wedged in the neck by means of a small rubber ball. That version, though effective, required some manipulation at the start and disposal of the hall at the finish, whereas this trick is automatic.

A special rope is used. It contains a thin rubber tube attached to a bulb which is hidden in the hand at the upper end. Within the rope, near the lower end, is a tiny bulb of much thinner rubber. When the magician secretly squeezes the large bulb, the tiny one inflates inside the rope and swells sufficiently to support the bottle which should be of lightweight plastic. When pressure on the large bulb is relaxed, the bottle drops free.

63

5. The Red Ribbon Pack

Effect: This mystery is quite a contrast to the usual form of card discoveries, as it involves a pack specially arranged to be threaded on a red ribbon. The pack does not have to consist of playing cards; in fact, those used for other types of games are preferable, since the pack is employed in this trick only.

The distinctive feature of the pack is that each card has a vertical slot cut up the center, running less than two-thirds the length of the card and measuring about a half inch in width. It is best to have these punched out by a die, so that the cards will be uniform. The purpose of this slot, which has a margin at each end, is to allow the entire sack to be strung upon a red ribbon a few feet in length.

Showing that the pack consists entirely of different cards, the magician allows one to be selected and returned. He gives the pack to be shuffled and later runs through the faces of the cards to show that the chosen one—known only to the person who drew it—is buried somewhere in the pack.

The pack is strung on the ribbon, the ends of which are held by spectators. Even then, the cards may be spread to show that the chosen one is not on the top or the bottom. With the pack hanging on the center of the ribbon, the magician covers it with a handkerchief, reaches beneath, and states that he will find the chosen card.

A few moments later, the magician draws a card face down from beneath the cloth, brings it along the ribbon and carries it from the end, which is released to allow the passage of the card. It proves, when shown, to be the chosen card. Ribbon and pack may then be examined with special stress upon the fact that no duplicate cards are used.

Method: The secret is quite ingenious, with a neat feature that makes the operation of the trick nearly automatic. There is no fakery whatever in the construction of the pack. It all depends on the length of the slot cut in the cards. The length of the slot is precisely the same as the actual width of each card. Moreover, the slot is not quite centered. It is punched so that it runs about a quarter-inch closer to one end of the pack than the other.

After a card has been removed, the magician turns the pack around. Thus, with the slots all set the same way beforehand, the chosen card will be reversed when it is replaced. This fact is not apparent until the pack is hanging from the ribbon, so the magician does not actually dangle it until he has covered the pack with the handkerchief or is about to do so.

65

CHOSEN CARD

CUT IN DECK OF CARDS
IS ¼ INCH CLOSER
AT ONE END.

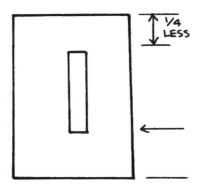

¼
LESS

Red Ribbon Pack

Thus the chosen card will project slightly from the others, either downward or upward. Downward is preferable, so the pack may be dangled freely without the projecting card being noticed. Under the handkerchief, the magician finds this card by its projecting end. Separating the pack at that point, he points the card crosswise and thrusts it through the slotted centers of either section of the back.

In drawing the card into sight along the ribbon, it should be held in a vertical position like the rest of the pack at that point, to avoid any clue to the method whereby it apparently penetrated its companions. Stiff cards are the best for a pack of this sort, as they can be shuffled without snagging the slots.

To make this trick up yourself you can use all thirteen cards from one suit instead of a complete deck.

6. The Patriotic Liquids

Effect: On a tray, the magician has a dozen small glasses containing what he terms "Patriotic Liquids." Four glasses hold a red liquid, four a colorless liquid which is used instead of white, while four are filled with a blue liquid.

Showing a tall, thin glass container of the type called a hydrometer jar, the magician next exhibits an empty tube of similar proportions. He sets the tube over the jar, then proceeds to pour the liquids into the covered jar.

First red, then the white (or colorless) and finally the blue. Glass by glass, the magician follows this rotation. He pours all the liquids slowly and carefully to insure the magical result. This is seen when the magician lifts the tube from the tall glass jar.

Method: Instead of the liquids being a darkish mixture, they appear in perfect layers, exactly as poured, running red, white, blue, and repeating that rotation three times, from the bottom of the jar to the top.

The secret is very neat. The red and blue liquids are chemically colored. The white, or colorless, contains oxalic acid, which is a bleaching agent. When the liquids are poured into the covered jar, they all become colorless. Inside the tube, however, is a snug-fitting cylinder of celluloid, painted with horizontal stripes of red and blue with a colorless space between.

The cylinder cannot be observed inside the tube when it is casually shown empty. After the pouring, when the tube is lifted, the celluloid tube is left around the jar, which it fits rather closely. This accounts for the "layers" of liquids which the spectators observe when the tube is lifted.

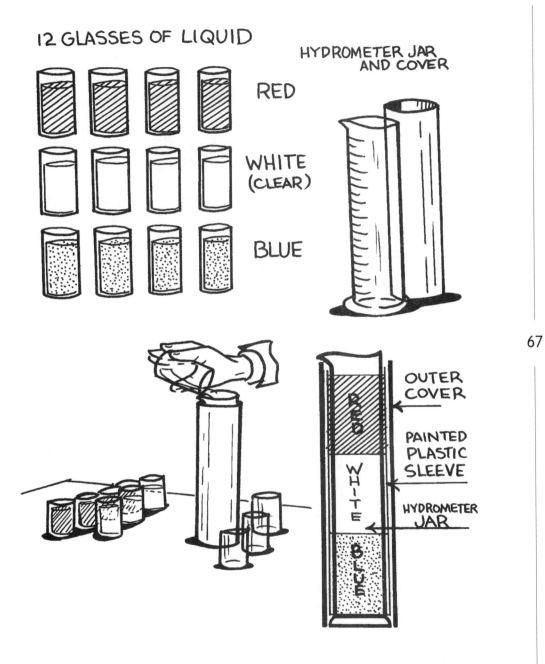

12 GLASSES OF LIQUID

RED

WHITE (CLEAR)

BLUE

HYDROMETER JAR AND COVER

OUTER COVER

PAINTED PLASTIC SLEEVE

HYDROMETER JAR

RED

WHITE

BLUE

Patriotic Liquids

Unlike most chemical effects, this trick is particularly baffling to chemists who witness it. They can understand how it could be done with liquids of different densities, but not to the extent of a dozen such. The unsuspected celluloid tube with its painted layers is the factor that makes this trick into a real mystery.

Be careful whenever dealing with chemicals. An adult should always supervise young children.

7. Card, Seal, and Ribbon

Effect: While essentially a card trick, this effect has the type of audience appeal that goes well with an act of varied magic, since articles other than the cards are required in its performance.

The magician hands someone a pack of cards, requesting that a card be drawn and that the person write his name across its face. The card is returned to about the center of the pack, which is turned face upward and cut. The card at which the magician cuts—say the Jack of Spades—obviously is not the selected card since it has nothing written upon it.

The magician takes a large gold seal which is attached to a ribbon. He sticks the seal on the corner of the face-up Jack of Spades, which is still resting on the pack, and has someone put his initials on the seal to verify it. With the pack still face up, the under half is cut and placed upon the Jack, thus burying, it.

Asking the person who chose the original card to name it, the magician learns its identity—say the Six of Diamonds. Giving the person the free end of the ribbon, he tells him to pull the Jack of Spades from the pack and have another look at it. The spectator does so; to his surprise, he finds that the card attached to the seal is now the Six of Diamonds, bearing his signature, and that the seal is the one with another spectator's initials.

Method: The trick depends on a "key card," in this case the Jack of Spades. The corner of the card at the outer left has been clipped off by using a finger nail clipper. Thus by riffling the pack at that corner, the magician can always stop at the Jack of Spades, as it leaves a sharp gap when it falls.

The chosen card, when replaced, goes directly upon the Jack of Spades. At this point, the pack is face down; the cards should be the sort that have a pattern running to the edge, with no white margin, so that the missing corner of the Jack will not be noticed.

68

Turning the pack face up, the magician cuts to the key card by riffling the outer corner, which is now at the right. Thus the Jack of Spades is face up, with the chosen Six of Diamonds just below it. The magician keeps his thumb over the missing corner of the Jack as he holds the pack.

The gold seal is attached to the ribbon by means of a small sticker, the end of the ribbon being glued between them. This of course has been prepared beforehand. The seal itself has no gum, but the smaller sticker is so provided. Hence in moistening the seal, the magician dampens the sticker only. The seal, when placed on the corner of the pack, covers over the missing corner of the face-up Jack. The sticker, however, does not touch the Jack, but fastens itself to the card beneath. When the pack is cut and the ribbon is pulled, the card that comes from the pack is the chosen one. While the spectators are identifying the signed card and the initialed seal, the magician scrambles to the key card, secretly removes it and drops it in his pocket. An unprepared Jack of Spades can already be in the pack in case any one asks to see the cards.

It's a really great effect. This is good for the expert or the beginner who wants to look like a pro.

Stage Effects That Can Be Purchased In Most Magic Shops

1. Thumb Tip

Effect: The magician shows both hands empty. Makes a fist with one hand and pulls a silk out of the fist. The magician hands the hanky around for inspection. The magician takes back the hanky, makes a fist, pokes the hanky back into the fist, and opens the hand to show that the hanky has vanished.

Method: This effect holds a special place in my heart since the first time I performed it at the tender age of 11. I'll never forget how wide my mother's eyes became when I opened my hand and showed that the silk had vanished. Like the Dye box mentioned earlier in the last section, the thumb tip is a magic utility device to make small objects such as silks, coins, sponge balls, etc. disappear and reappear. The Thumb tip is a plastic fake thumb that goes over your actual thumb

To perform the effect above you have prepare by load a small silk into your thumb tip and place the thumb tip on your thumb (I typically wear the thumb tip on my left hand). Show both hands empty. Make a fist with your right hand. Then stick your thumb into the fist as if you're trying to pull the silk out with your thumb. As you do this, drop the thumb tip into your fist. As you pull out your thumb also pull out a little piece of the silk. Use your left fingers to pull out the rest of the silk simultaneously placing the thumb tip back on your thumb.

To make the silk disappear, make a fist around your left thumb and drop the thumb tip into it. Then poke the silk into the thumb tip pretending to poke it into the fist. Take turns between your thumb and index finger when poking. When the entire silk is in the thumb tip, poke your thumb into the thumb tip pulling it out of the fist. Do one last poke with your left index finger into the fist and then show that the silk has vanished.

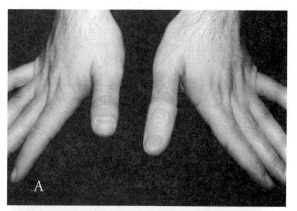

A

Tips:

•Every magician at some point or another has owned a thumb tip. I highly recommend purchasing one and with it buy a book that teaches multiple effects with the tip. I believe there is a book out called *101 Tricks to do with a Thumb Tip*.

•There are many thumb tips on the market. I prefer using the ones that are made out of a softer rubber as opposed to a hard plastic. Try to find one that most closely matches the color

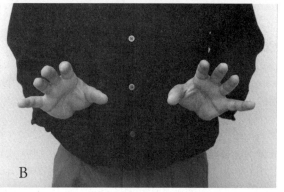

B

of your skin, but I want to give you fair warning that none will totally match. Not to worry, I once saw a black magician fool people with a white thumb tip.

When showing your hands empty point your thumbs toward the audience –it makes it even more difficult to detect the thumb tip. In the picture you can barely tell that I am wearing the thumb tip on my left thumb. The way to perfect using a thumb tip is to where one. I wore one constantly for a month in a half without ever performing an effect. I wanted to see if anybody noticed it. Not only did I gain confidence in realizing that nobody these days pays attention to detail, but I also got comfortable wearing the apparatus.

Perhaps the most important tip of all is how to properly fit a thumb tip to your thumb. The thumb tip should not be fit all the way down your thumb. It should stop at around the first bending point (a quarter of an inch below the nail).(**Pic A**). Although you may feel like your thumb is way too long, do not worry. The audience will never notice. Did you notice that I was wearing a thumb tip inthe picture in the Introduction? (**Refer to Page xvii**). The worst thing you can do is buy an oversized thumb tip that falls off your thumb during performance.

2. Adhesive Milk

Effect: An ordinary milk bottle is shown partly filled with milk. Placing a sheet of paper over the mouth of the bottle, the magician clamps his hand upon it and inverts the bottle. He peels away the sheet of paper and the milk remains transfixed in the bottle.

The milk is real enough, for the spectators can see its new level in the bottle, now that the bottle has been inverted. The problem is: What can be holding it there? There is only one answer—Magic! To prove this, the magician takes a long, thin metal skewer and pushes it up through the mouth of the bottle. The end of the skewer appears above the level of the milk.

This process is repeated several times, and finally the milk is poured from the bottle into a pitcher. At any time, the magician can cause the remaining milk to cling within the bottle when the latter is turned upside down.

Method: The trick is accomplished with the aid of a simple disk made of wire screen, its edge bordered with a thin strip. This disk is inserted in the neck of the bottle, being made to fit there snugly. When the bottle is inverted, the milk will not flow through the screen, because the holes are too small to admit sufficient air.

In brief, the wire fake acts exactly like the sheet of paper that the magician first placed across the mouth of the bottle and then removed.

The convincing part takes place when the magician pushes the thin skewer up into the bottle. All he needs is a skewer thinner than the holes in the screen. He can push it up and down as he pleases, simply stabbing through the openwork of the wire mesh.

When the bottle is tilted at an angle, air is admitted and the milk will flow out through the screen, but as soon as it is brought back to the vertical, the milk will stay in the bottle.

A neat way to introduce this trick is to have the bottle covered with a regular milk cap or top. The bottle is full of milk and can be opened under the noses of the spectators because the screen disk is deep in the top of the bottle proper, and therefore hidden by the milk.

Covering the bottle with the paper, the magician inverts it, holds it over a pitcher and peels away the paper. The small surplus of milk drops from the top of the bottle in very convincing style, while the rest of the milk remains. The magician then slants the bottle, pours out some of the milk, and covers the bottle with the paper again. He peels away the paper, the bottle remains half full, and the demonstration is made with the skewer, as earlier described.

The modern presentation of this trick is done with a clear plastic gimmick with a hole in it that fits over the mouth of a soda or beer bottle. It is easy to find.

3. Disecto

Effect: The wave of "torture illusions" that came into popularity some years ago have found their counterpart in smaller effects, suited for the platform. Thus, instead of chopping a girl piecemeal and then restoring her—as will be explained in a later chapter—magicians are sometimes content to perform such operations on a smaller or restricted scale.

It is not commonly known that these lesser effects in the department were originally intended as preliminary demonstrations leading up to the stage illusions themselves. Such was the case, and several excellent small effects were designed for such purpose only to be discarded because they took something of the interest from the larger effects that followed.

However, out of such experimental work developed a group of smaller torture effects that are fine for the club and platform worker, because of their portability. In such a category come the "choppers" or miniature guillotines, one type of which is herewith described and explained, under the appropriate title of "The Gay Blade."

This device consists of a block or frame, built like a thin stand and mounted on a pedestal. The frame is made in two sections, so that a sharp blade like a cleaver can be slashed from top to bottom within the halves of the frame. One end of the blade

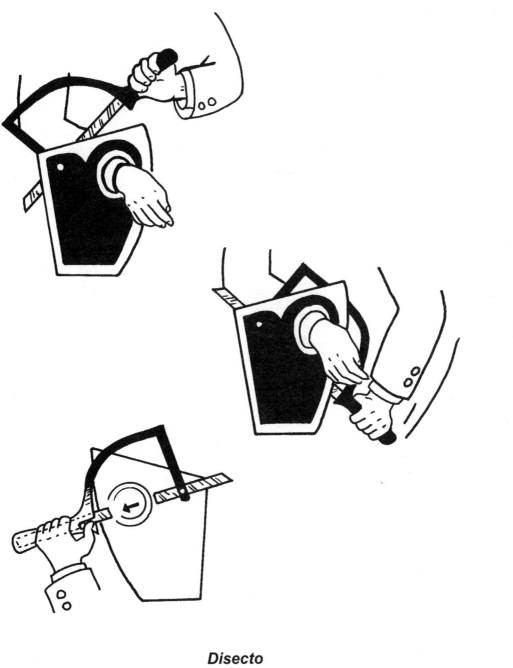

Disecto

is pivoted to the frame itself; at the other end of the blade is a handle, so that when swung downward, the handle describes a long arc.

Midway in the double frame is a hole large enough for the insertion of a person's wrist. A victim is selected from the audience and watches while the magician swings the blade downward, through and past the hole. To show that the blade is really sharp, the magician puts a carrot in the hole and cuts it in half with a sweep of the blade. Then the person from the audience is invited to insert his wrist. He does so and the magician gives the blade another downward slash, right through the wrist, which is promptly removed, still on the arm and quite unharmed.

The trick is convincing because the pivoted end of the blade projects from beyond the frame. Also the portion of the blade that apparently cleaves the wrist can be seen above the frame when the blade is raised; below after it has made the chop. Yet despite this, the blade never contacts the wrist.

Method: This is because the pivoted end of the blade is simply a dummy. It is connected with the handle by means of a large curved rod that circles up above the frame and over to the handle, apparently nothing more than a special support to keep the long blade from wavering during its down-sweep. Thus the part of the blade that sweeps through the wrist-hole is actually a short length connected to the handle.

The handle itself is long and hollow on the side away from the spectators. At the handle end of the fake blade is a knob that the magician can engage with his thumb. When he is ready to "chop" the person's wrist, he brings the handle down just far enough to hide the blade in the slit between the frames, then draws the short blade into the handle with his thumb, releasing it the instant he has chopped past the wrist, so that the full blade appears in the space below the frame.

This trick is now being made by Abotts in Colon, Michigan and by Supreme Magic in England. (This trick was called the Gay Blade.)

4. The Penetrating Liquids

Effect: Taking a bottle of colored soda water, the magician pours its contents into a tall metal can that narrows from bottom to top and is furbished with an outward slanting rim. On this he places a sheet of glass, upon which he sets an inverted funnel.

Gripping the can with one hand, the handle of the funnel with the other, he turns them over, pressing the glass firmly between. He sets the tip of the funnel in the empty bottle, holding the glass sheet steady so that the can remains inverted upon it.

Naturally, the liquid does not escape from the can because the glass prevents it. The magician is then ready to perform a minor miracle. He commands the liquid to penetrate the glass. Instantly, the liquid begins to flow from the funnel until it fills the bottle. Lifting the can from the glass, the magician rattles a wand inside it, showing that the liquid is really gone and therefore must have penetrated the sheet of glass.

Method: This is a clever combination of two special devices. One is called the "Foo Can" because it was first introduced by the Chinese magician, Ching Ling Foo. This can has a slanted partition running from one side of the top to the other side of the bottom, inside the can. There is a space, however, at the bottom of the partition.

When the liquid is poured into the can, the magician has only to invert the latter in the proper direction and the liquid—which only half fills the can—will go into the hidden compartment and remain there. This accounts for the can's being empty at the finish.

The funnel is also tricked. It is actually a double funnel, one within the other, the outer funnel tapering more sharply than the inner. Under the handle of the funnel is a tiny air-hole which is covered with a bit of gummed cellophane tape after the double funnel is filled with liquid, which is done beforehand.

By loosening the tape with his fingernail, the magician causes the hidden liquid to flow from the funnel into the bottle, giving the illusion that it has penetrated the sheet of glass from the can above.

5. Vanishing Candle

Effect: The magician displays a silk. He then picks up a 13 or 14 inch lit candle and blows out the flame. He covers the candle and in an instant the candle vanishes from under the silk.

Method: Fantasio developed a retractable candle made out of plastic . When the candle is pulled out to it's full length it can be up to 14 inches in length, and when it retracts it's only a mere inch and a half. The candle stays in it's full length when pressure is applied to the bottom of the candle. By releasing the pressure the candle collapses into itself . Inside the candle there is a small metal cylinder that holds lighter fluid and a wick. This is what allows for the candle to be lit on fire. Fantasio's vanishing candle can also be performed as a reappearing candle by pulling the candle out to it's full length under a silk. Then the same candle can be made to vanish by releasing the pressure and allowing it to retract under the silk. Although Fantasio also sells a reappearing candle that springs open and is easier to use for a production than the vanishing candle. Any decent magic shop should own either of these apparatus or be able to order it for you.

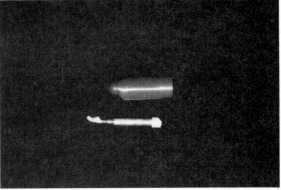

76

This effect is typically not performed in and of itself but combined with other effects. For example, Lance Burton typically produces a few candles and then makes one vanish and turn into a dove. I use this effect in almost every show I perform, but I do lots of stage shows. This apparatus is not too effective in close-up and should only really be purchased if you think you'll be performing it on stage or if you just like collecting cool apparatus at a costly price. Finally although it is a gimmick that sounds simple to use, this effect is considered difficult sleight of hand and needs much practice to perform well.

6. Sands of Sahara

Effect: Showing two shallow metal pans, shaped like oversized saucers, the magician calls attention to the fact that one is filled with sand, which he states is direct from the Sahara desert. Pouring the sand back and forth from pan to pan, the performer adds that it would really take a magician to cause anything to grow in such a dry substance.

Bringing the pans mouth to mouth, the magician sets them on a small stand or pedestal. A few magic words, then the pans are lifted and spread apart, each coming mouth upward. Instead of sand each pan is filled with a blooming bouquet of colorful desert flowers.

Method: Each pan has a circular depression in the bottom. Over one lies a metal disk painted like the interior of the pan. Attached to the under side of the disk is a bunch of expanding flowers made of paper. A similar bunch is attached to the pan itself. A pin runs through the side of the pan, holding the disk in place.

After pouring a small quantity of sand back and forth, the magician leaves the pan with the hidden flowers on the top of the pair when they are placed mouth to mouth. He pulls the pin in setting the pans on the stand and the disk drops to the lower pan, covering the sand which has sifted down to its depressed bottom.

The top pan is quickly turned upright and the flowers spring wide, filling both pans. These paper flowers are equipped with double-spreading springs, so that they can be packed compactly, yet will make a large display when opened.

Known as "Spring Flowers," they were invented by the famous magician, Buatier de Kolta, who also invented the celebrated "Vanishing Bird Cage" and a series of brilliant stage illusions. Simple though the construction of the flowers was, it didn't impress magicians until during one of de Kolta's performances some of the flowers fluttered out into the audience.

From these samples, thousands of duplicates were made and sold to magicians. Today they are listed as accessories in nearly every dealer's catalog and are purchased in lots of twenty-five or more.

This trick is now history, but the spring flowers have remained and are a part of many magicians' bag of tricks.

77

7. Eggs From the Hat

Effect: Inviting a boy and girl from the audience, the magician shows an empty hat. From it he begins to produce eggs, handing them to the girl and instructing her to give them to the boy. More and more eggs keep coming from the hat. Soon the boy's arms are so laden with eggs that he can scarcely hold them.

The eggs then begin to drop. The girl becomes so busy placing the eggs in the boy's arms and steadying those already there that she enters into the spirit

FALSE BOTTOM

Eggs From The Hat

of confusion. Meanwhile the magician is blandly producing eggs in inexhaustible style. At last, the remaining eggs are salvaged and the trick brought to a mysterious as well as laughable conclusion.

Method: Presentation is the essential factor in this trick. The hat is a special one of double construction, with an inner lining that conceals the eggs, which are packed all around the interior. Through an opening in the lining, the magician draws out the eggs, depending upon the quantity of the eggs to give the mystery its zest.

The "Eggs and Hat" was a specialty with the Great Raymond, who performed it throughout the world. Raymond's rendition was particularly artistic because of the way in which he kept passing the eggs along to the girl, who failed to see the next egg as she reached for it, in her anxiety to make sure that the boy did not drop the heap that was precariously balanced in his arms. Thus the girl, not the boy, was the one who dropped the eggs and at the finish, Raymond would carefully work the eggs from the boy's arms back into the hat, so skillfully that the audience would gain the amazed impression that more eggs had been produced than the hat itself could have held.

This was real artistry in contrast to the way in which many performers worked the act, their procedure being to hurry the boy into dropping so many eggs that the stage was spattered with them. This was an inferior presentation, as it reduced the trick to a comedy number and nothing more.

In Raymond's hands, the "Eggs and Hat" soon became a feature of his show and stands out as a striking example of magical accomplishment.

With the passing of popularity of men's hats, you can use a plastic hat available at the party stores or even a paper bag (see illustration). This is not a trick to try in your parents' living room!

8. Fade-Away Glass

Effect: This mystery was a favorite with David Devant, the famous English illusionist, who performed many of his marvels in a deliberate and convincing style which added to the mystification of the audience. It illustrates how a comparatively small trick can be built to a strong magical climax.

The magician shows a large glass, considerably larger than the average tumbler. He fills it with water, covers it with a cloth, and approaches the footlights. At this point, the audience expects the glass to be vanished from the

79

handkerchief, but the magician is not so abrupt about it.

Coming down the steps into the audience, the magician lets them hold the glass within the handkerchief, making sure that it is really there. He taps the glass through the cloth and people hear its muffled ring.

By now, everyone is impressed by the fact that the glass is quite a large one, since people themselves have handled it. Obviously it would be quite a task for the magician to conjure away such a sizable glass of water in the midst of his audience. When he places his hands beneath the handkerchief, every one supposes that the magician merely intends to bring out the glass and give the spectators another look at it before returning to the stage.

Instead, the magician suddenly whisks away the handkerchief and the glass is gone. He tosses the handkerchief for examination, shows his hands completely empty, takes a bow and returns to the stage, leaving every one with the impression that the glass literally faded away.

Method: There is an adage that "nothing should be done by halves" but the rule does not apply in magic. The glass used in this trick is actually of double thickness, consisting of a bottomless outer cylinder around a straight-walled glass. After filling the apparently normal glass with water, the magician covers it with the cloth and lets the inner glass drop into a bag behind a table, the water going with it.

Thus the glass that the spectators feel beneath the cloth is only the outer cylinder, but it is of the right size to pass as the glass. When the magician places his hands beneath the handkerchief, the large size of the cylinder proves a help, not a handicap, for he is able to slide it over one hand and well up his arm, beneath his sleeve. That is the last place where the audience would suspect a large glass to go, particularly as they suppose it to be filled with water. Thus the rapid vanish is as baffling as it is unexpected.

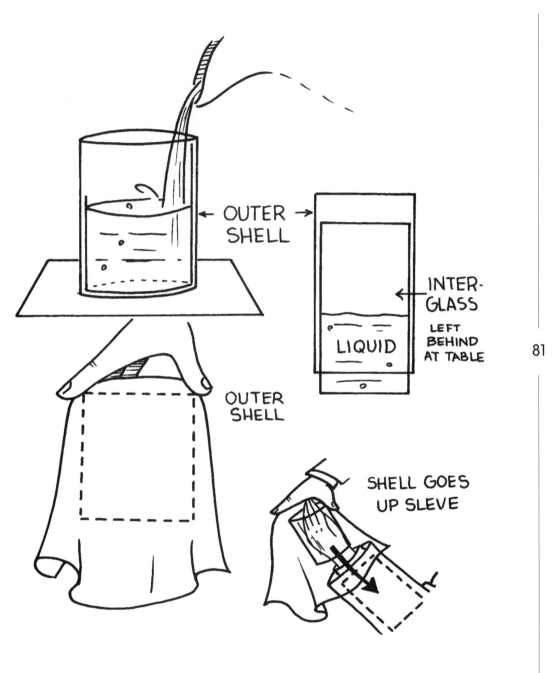

OUTER SHELL

INTER-GLASS

LEFT BEHIND AT TABLE

LIQUID

OUTER SHELL

SHELL GOES UP SLEVE

Fade-Away Glass

9. The Great Sack Escape

Effect: Escape tricks come under the head of stage effects, although they may be performed in various other places, even at the bottom of rivers. However, they figure in a magical show only as a special added attraction, because it is difficult to estimate the time they will take. They are more in the category of a challenge than that of strict entertainment.

To perform escapes requires a great deal of practice and foresight, for the work is both arduous and dangerous, and is suitable only to the practicing professional who must find some way to advertise his show through sensational publicity. Such performers will find all sorts of people challenging them to escape from anything from bank vaults to refrigerators. Such feats can become quite troublesome and strenuous, though often some very imposing escapes prove far less difficult than they appear.

Since escapes are useful only to a limited number of performers, there is no purpose in going into a catalog of complicated devices. What the average performer needs is a good escape that impresses his audience, yet avoids danger as well as the necessity of carrying bulky paraphernalia. Hence "The Great Sack Escape" is recommended, particularly because it is as easy of performance as it is ingenious in method.

The performer introduces a large black sack, which may be thoroughly examined. He is placed in the sack and a borrowed handkerchief is tied around the neck as proof that the performer cannot cut the bonds that hold him, since the handkerchief is to be identified later. Next, ropes are tied around the neck of the sack above the handkerchief; to identify these, they may be sealed with wax.

The performer is then placed in a cabinet. After a short interval, he appears before the audience, carrying the sack, with the knotted handkerchief and the sealed and knotted ropes still intact around the neck.

Method: To work this mystery, two sacks are required. They are identical in appearance and it is best to have them made of fairly thin material, because they must be packed in small space. At the outset, the performer has one of these sacks folded and tucked under his coat. The other sack is examined by the audience and the magician gets into it.

82

The magician has an assistant helping him and here is where the assistant's work comes in. The assistant gathers up the neck of the sack, holding it rather loosely and starts to tie a borrowed handkerchief around it. By then, the performer has removed the duplicate sack from beneath his coat. He thrusts the neck of the duplicate up through that of the original sack.

Adjusting the sack necks, the assistant ties the handkerchief tightly around the spot where they join. The sacks being black or of other dark material, this trickery with the necks is not observed and the handkerchief hides the join adequately. The assistant keeps pulling it tighter while spectators—brought on stage as a committee—tie ropes around the neck of the sack above the join. Actually they are tying their ropes around the duplicate sack—not the original. These are the ropes that are later sealed.

To all appearances the magician is tightly imprisoned in the sack. Once he is placed within a cabinet or behind a screen, he has no trouble with his escape. He simply peels away the outer sack (the original) leaving the handkerchief as well as the ropes tied around the duplicate. Folding the original sack, he tucks it under his coat, hiding it as the duplicate was hidden in the first place. Then the performer makes his appearance before the puzzled audience, bringing along the duplicate sack, which can stand any amount of examination.

This escape must be well rehearsed beforehand and care must be taken in handling the committee, as is true with the majority of escapes. Those precautions taken, "The Great Sack Escape" will prove to capital mystery. As an escape it will be found well suited to a magical show because it can be performed quite rapidly, without the long stage waits that have made many escape tricks too slow and tedious for presentation before modern audiences.

10. Duck or Rabbit Box Production

Effect: The production of two or three live ducks from an empty box is always a sensational effect. Where the ducks come from is a problem to the audience; how to keep them there until their appearance is the magician's problem. This type of box answers both problems satisfactorily.

Picking up an oblong box with an overlapping top and bottom, the magician grips a handle on the top and lets the box drop wide open. The front side of the box is hinged to the top, the bottom of the box is hinged to the rear side. Thus the box opens accordion fashion, letting the audience see clear through it.

The Great Sack Escape

The box is closed by simply raising the bottom upward, gathering the box proper and clamping the lid shut. When the magician opens two doors in the top, the ducks appear and hop out, quacking loudly, to waddle across the stage.

Method: In the description of the box, we find the answer. Apparently the box is shown entirely empty; actually, it is not. Attached within the top of the box is a container, almost as large as the box itself. In opening the box, the magician swings the top forward and outward; thus the container can not be seen. When he lifts the box, the hinged center drops and from it dangles the bottom. The eyes of the spectator follow the dropping box and observe that nothing is concealed in the main portion or the bottom.

Nobody suspects the innocent looking top behind which the ducks are concealed in their container. In closing the box, the magician takes care to bring the bottom up toward the top, which is allowed to settle in place without revealing the load behind it. The reason for the double doors in the top is now plain. Upon release, the ducks come out of their container, through the top of the box.

A few more details should be noted. The doors in the top should fit neatly, one having a strip that overlaps the other so that the ducks cannot be glimpsed, Also, the doors should be held together by a catch, so that the ducks cannot force them open too soon. Those points observed, the trick is certain of operation.

This box can also be made in smaller size for the production of a rabbit or other objects Such as silk handkerchiefs and spring flowers. When made in smaller proportions, a single door in the top is quite as effective as a double door. It should, of course, be a good fit and have a catch.

The beauty of this production lies in the bold, direct handling of the box. The magician should simply pick it up by the handle, which is attached to one of the doors (or the single door in the case of a smaller box). If picked up from a tray or table, the box opens automatically. If the magician holds his other hand beneath it, he can let the box drop apart whenever he chooses. A good clear view convinces the audience that the box is entirely empty and the magician has only to close the box and proceed with the production.

Since its inception, this same box with two holes, one on one on each side of the box, it has been used mainly for vanishes and is called a "flip-over" box.

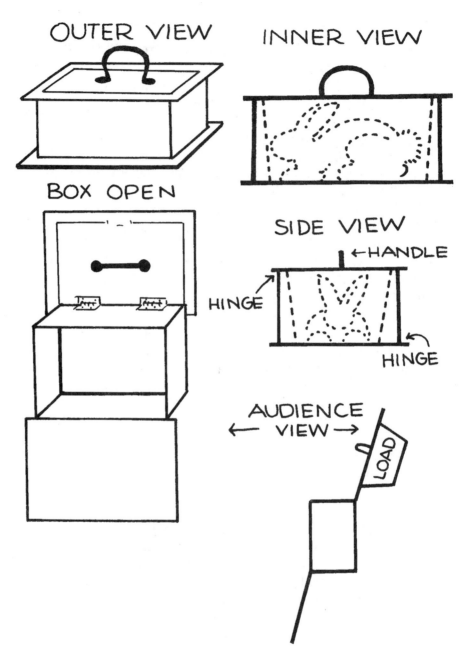

Duck or Rabbit Box Production

11. Pop Thru Frame

Effect: This is a production trick with a surprise feature. Devised by Milbourne Christopher, it is an example of portability in equipment, enabling magicians to carry considerable apparatus in small space.

An assistant brings on a large square frame which the magician covers with a sheet of paper. As the magician calls upon the audience to name colors, the paper punctures itself automatically and through the hole pops a large silk handkerchief of the first color called.

This is repeated, colored silks arriving from nowhere in the order given by the audience. The wizard can also cause flags of various nations to make their "pop-through" appearance as demanded.

Method: Over his right hand, the assistant wears a hollow dummy hand, which he attaches to the side of the frame. Inside his vest or jacket, the handkerchiefs, flags or both are arranged in careful order. The frame is quite large, extending at least a foot on each side of the assistant. The assistant can draw his right hand, unseen, from within the hollow dummy.

While the left hand alone supports the lightly constructed frame, the hidden right reaches into the vest, draws the required silk from its place and gathers it against the back of the paper. The finger punches the silk through the paper, causing it to pop into sight, the finger being gone from view before the silk drops clear. Other silks are similarly produced, as called. At the finish, the right hand slides back into the dummy.

Easier than a fake hand would be the use of a thumb or a dye tube. These are both easy to obtain.

87

12. Twentieth Century Silks

Effect: The magician vanishes a blue silk. He then pulls out two red silks which are tied together and shoved down a volunteers shirt (you probably want to choose a male volunteer for this trick, just to be on the safe side) so that the two free ends are sticking out of the shirt. The magician pulls on one end while a second volunteer pulls on the other end, and the blue silk pops out of the shirt tied between the two red silks.

Method: The twentieth century silks are a classic of magic. Adaptations have been made to this effect where two silks are tied and stuffed into a gentleman's pants, and when they are pulled out his underwear is tied between them. The Twentieth Century silks works because one of the red silks is actually sewn in half at a diagonal leaving a hollow space between them. To one corner of the rigged red silk a corner of the blue silk is sewn. In this same corner of the red silk a slit allows for the blue silk to be tucked into the hollow part of the red silk. The opposite end of the blue silk is colored red and sticks out of the slit so that when the two corners of the red silks are tied it is actually the corner of one red and one blue silk. Thus, when the opposite corners of the red silks are pulled, they pull the blue silk out of the rigged red silk.

In the effect described above, the duplicate can be made to disappear in a number of ways. You can use a change bag, thumb tip, or die box. Once you have made the duplicate vanish the rest is acting and playing with your audience member. Typically magicians bring up a volunteer and say that the blue silk which vanished has reappeared beneath the volunteer's shirt. Then pretending to be disgusted about going under the volunteer's shirt, the magician says I'll have these two silks go get it. Then the routine is completed by performing the twentieth century silks.

Part 4

Mysticism and Mentalism

I have combined mysticism and mentalism because they are extremely similar in theory and the effects can be performed as either mystical effects or mental effects. Essentially the effects are interchangeable depending on how you want to present them. Speaking of presentation the two key concepts to keep in mind when performing all of these effects is (1) (as mentioned in the introduction) the magic occurs in the viewer's mind, and (2) Setting the mood.

Keeping Magic in Mind

As I mentioned in the introduction, magic occurs in your audience's mind and not in your hands. This maxim holds especially true for mysticism and mentalism. The method for having the audience create the magic in their minds is simply to provide them with suggestions in which they come up with the conclusion that what you are doing can only be accomplished by supernatural means. I once saw a mentalist who started his act by asking everyone, "Have you ever heard the phone ring and you knew who it was before you answered it. You can't explain why but when you picked up the phone the person you were thinking of was on the other line. The demonstrations I'll be performing for you are based on much of the same principles." Here the magician suggest, and does so quite subtly, that we all have the power of intuition and that power can be developed so that you seem to have supernatural capabilities. But this suggestion turns into a conclusion in the audiences' minds. I believe the closest thing to true magic is the power of suggestion. It is much easier to mislead a spectator into coming up with their own false conclusions than it is to prove to them that the fantastical is real.

Setting the Mood

So how does one harness the power of suggestion? It's all about setting the mood. Setting the mood has a profound impact on people. It can make them feel romantic, silly, serious, etc. Your lighting, music, props, and even voice all play a part in setting the mood. Hence the reason seances are often performed in the dark or in candlelight. Setting the mood allows for the audience to loose themselves which in turn allows them to accept your suggestions. Once you have tapped into the mind of a spectator and broken through their locks of skepticism you can get them to believe almost anything.

Little History of Mysticism

For a period, the "Midnite Spook Show," pervaded the magical scene with its thrills, chills, and everything else from glamour ghouls to vanishing vampires. This type of entertainment has to a great degree supplanted the lesser road shows that once played the local opera houses, but despite their emphasis on the weird, the better Ghost Shows are actually magical extravaganzas condensed to an hour's length. Spooky effects are sprinkled through the act and the windup is a "blackout" that fulfills all the qualifications of the old-time spirit seance.

This represents an interesting evolution. A century ago, there occurred the now-famous "Rochester Rappings" in a house near that city, which caused the gullible public to believe that there might be a ghost in every home. Soon a group of itinerant performers were capitalizing on the craze, most notably the Davenport Brothers, Ira and Erasmus, who presented an act that had the public guessing, not only in America but abroad.

Bound with ropes, in a four-sided opaque screened area approximately 5 feet wide by 5 feet long by 7 feet high, the Davenports caused all sorts of spooky things to happen. Guitars strummed, bells were pitched through windows of the cabinet. Their show ended with a dark seance in which ghosts floated out over the audience. The consensus of opinion in that day was that the Davenports had genuine psychic powers, whereas actually they were skilled at getting in and out of ropes. Today, catalogs of knots and splices feature the "Davenport Knot" as a type that can be slipped or tightened as desired. Also such volumes classify a "Tom Fool's Knot" which closely resembles the "Davenport Knot" and was invented to trick the famous brothers during their tour of England.

As a boy, Harry Kellar traveled with the Davenports. Later, when he became the Great Kellar, the leading magician in America, he included a rope-tie in his program. Kellar also used Spook Cabinets in his performance and a Kellar Cabinet was a feature of the Thurston show. Blackstone became a specialist with the rope-tie and his performance of this mystery has rivaled that of Kellar. It was Blackstone, too, who introduced "Spook Nights" as special attractions with his regular show. All this coincided with the steady enlightenment of the public in regard to magic. Its recognition as skilled artistry applied to purposes of entertainment increased the popularity of magic and diminished belief in the supernatural claims, which performers like the Davenports once intimated were theirs (even though they may not have openly avowed them). The same applies to other kinds of spookery which were constantly duplicated and eventually taken over by magicians from the purveyors of the pseudo-psychic.

Thus the midnight shows which begin with a display of streamlined magic and climax with a series of ghostly gambols are accepted by the public in the same mood with which they view the horror movies that accompany such performances. The chilling moments are interspersed with spots of comedy relief that add up to good entertainment.

Chief credit for creating this vogue goes to Neff the Magician, who toured the country billed as "Doctor Neff and his Madhouse of Mystery," reviving interest in magical entertainment along with the thrills of the Spook Show. The dramatic quality which Neff has added to the presentation of magic has rated him among the "greats" in the art.

Neff's finale consists of a medley of "dark seance" effects in which his entire company participates, thus producing a mass of ghostly manifestations. Just as stage illusions represent magical methods scaled to the size needed for the theater, so do spook shows have a direct relation to the dispirit" effects that are frequently performed in more limited surroundings.

The tricks in this section all belong in the spook category, from impromptu effects through those which require a darkened seance room, and up to more elaborate presentations designed for the stage. Some performers specialize entirely in such effects, but usually the spook tricks are introduced as individual features in a magical routine.

Sometimes the lesser feats are performed as byplay with the other effects. This often depends upon the size of the group witnessing the performance. The "dark room" and "cabinet" effects are the sort that once were used by pretended mediums and in some instances can be traced back to such origins. But the closely guarded secrets that once belonged to the fraudulent fraternity could scarcely compete with the modern magical methods that have been applied to the development of spook tricks.

Much has been written of Daniel Home and other celebrated mediums who flourished a few generations ago. Could they drop around today to witness a first-class job of magical spookery, they would be the most baffled members of the audience.

Little Background on Mentalism

The latest development in the realm of the mysterious is that of "Mental Magic" which has also been publicized under the high-sounding title of "Mentalism" with the performer termed a "Mentalist" instead of a mere magician. Various factors have been responsible for this, so to give the reader a perspective of the subject, they will be treated here in brief.

Originally, mental effects were introduced in an act styled "Second Sight" wherein a magician glanced at objects proffered to him by members of the audience and called upon a blindfolded assistant to name them, which was done with surprising accuracy. Codes, signals and other systems of secret communication were utilized in this type of magic by various famous magicians until finally performers appeared upon the scene who specialized in such work only.

Most notable of such performers were the Zancigs, who titled their act "Two Minds with but a Single Thought" and astounded scientists and other investigators throughout the world. The Zancigs so elaborated their work that it was undetectable even by persons acquainted with the ordinary systems. Thus the Zancigs set the pattern for present-day "two person" acts which have been developed even further and require months and even years of practice and performance to approach perfection.

For a long while, the "Second Sight" act appealed chiefly to the intellectual members of a magician's audience. This was because a surprising percentage of the population, particularly in isolated districts, were inclined to accept many of the illusions that they witnessed on the stage as something akin to real wizardry. When Harry Kellar was bold enough to depict imps and demons on his lithographs, he did so in the face of arguments that such advertising would scare away a considerable percentage of the public. Even Howard Thurston, who succeeded Kellar and used similar billing, received complaints from persons (who were daring despite their superstitions) on the ground that devils did not appear in the show as pictured.

Feeling the public was sufficiently educated to accept magic as an art, legitimate magicians emphasized their skill at sleight-of-hand and described their stage effects as "illusions," even soft-pedaling their ever-popular Spook Cabinets as "anti-spiritualistic phenomena." The public, still wanting to believe in the impossible or miraculous, began to accept "Second Sight" as something psychic, since neither skill nor mechanics seemed capable of explaining it.

This led to a high-pressure type of performance that was practically the hokum of the crystal seer's parlor transferred to the theater. Self-styled "Mind Readers" sprang up in abundance and flourished through the vaudeville era. Foremost in this cavalcade was the celebrated Annie Eva Fay, whose act was extensively copied and elaborated. In such performances, questions are gathered from the audience, burned or otherwise destroyed, after which the mind reader "sees" the questions in the crystal and gives the answers.

Either the questions are "switched" for dummies, or facts are gained through the use of pads prepared to give the equivalent of carbon impressions. In any case, they are listed for the mind reader and supplied to him along with his crystal or by a variety of other devices. Through stooges or local informants, the act is given exaggerated proportions and the main purpose is to delude the gullible.

In contrast, the "mental tricks" performed by magicians come under the head of legitimate entertainment. This was the case with their "anti-spiritualistic phenomena" of years ago. But the very public which now regards such things as "Spirit Slate Writing" as nothing more than trickery, is charmingly inclined to grant supernormal ability to the purveyors of so-called "mental tests" that depend upon strictly magical methods.

This is simply the result of catch-phrase education. Wiseacres watching a magician will say, "Up his sleeve," or "It's done with mirrors," to explain away the disappearance of anything from a coin to an elephant. The actual case is that modern science and invention have managed to beat home the fact that physical impossibilities do not happen. But the marvels of the mind are still unexplored and the easiest way for ignorant persons to explain some feat of mental wizardry is to accept it as genuine.

The vast majority of observers never analyze magical effects beyond the point of guesswork. Otherwise they would recognize that the skilled sleight-of-hand man, who can vanish a coin before their eyes, might just as readily pluck a written question from an envelope without detection. They won't believe the magician who says that through some hypnotic power gained in India, he is literally able to saw a woman in half without harming her. But they will ,swallow the mentalist's patter when he declares that by tuning in on thought waves, he can gain impressions from concentrating minds.

Mental magic is therefore best suited for impromptu performances or fair-sized audiences. With the latter, the performer can often work his impromptu tests with the aid of a committee. In many instances, the performer concentrates upon mystifying individuals, counting upon their bewilderment to impress the audience as a whole, a factor which must be played up always. This is not different from other magic; often a magician will borrow a coin or a watch from a spectator, vanish it, and have it reappear to be identified solely by the owner. But with mental tricks, working for individuals is as much the rule as the exception.

Contrarily, the major purpose is to produce a mass amazement. To achieve this, a performer may often turn a stranger into a temporary confederate, letting him in on the secret of a trick—or a part of it—in order to astound the audience at large. Such subterfuge has been used with other types of magic, but very rarely. However, it has long been professional policy not to worry about a few persons catching on to a trick if everyone else is baffled.

Mysticism and Mentalism Effects

1. The Spirit Answer

Effect: Stating the spirits are ready to answer suitable questions, the performer takes a pad of paper and inserts a sheet of carbon between the two top leaves. He asks some one to write a question on the top sheet, asking, "Are you ready to answer questions?" Under the question the person is told to sign his name.

Tearing the sheet from the pad, the performer removes the carbon paper and shows the second sheet. There is the carbon writing, but for some uncanny reason, the wording has been changed. Instead of the question, the statement appears: "This certifies that the spooks can answer questions." Underneath the statement—and this is the puzzling part—appears the carbon copy of the person's signature.

Method: This is an excellent impromptu spook trick, depending on a neat device. The carbon paper is just slightly larger than the pad, to all appearances, but actually, it is about one-half longer. That extra length is folded under very carefully and creased to make it appear as the edge. That is the "edge" which is pushed up to the top of the pad, between the first two sheets.

The answer is already on the second sheet, written there through carbon paper. When the question is written on the top sheet, it is not transcribed, because two layers of carbon are face to face. But the signature, being written lower, is reproduced through the single carbon.

Several ordinary sheets of carbon paper should be handy, all cut to the approximate size of the pad. The folded carbon is picked as if at random, replaced with the others after the trick and can be slipped from the batch later.

94

2. Hanky Panky with Hyrum the Friendly Ghost

Effect: The magician pulls out a handkerchief and waves it around claiming this is a method for catching a ghost or some other mumbo jumbo like that. At that moment the magician makes a great gesture that implies he has caught the ghost. He then quickly folds the hanky as if to trap the ghost inside, but the hanky begins to move and rise. The magician quickly flattens the hanky but it still continues to jump. A person from the audience can even be allowed to feel the ghost move through the hanky. The magician tosses the hanky in the air and allows the ghost to go free.

Method: This effect is done by sewing a thin wire into the hem of a handkerchief from one corner to the midpoint of one of the sides. The end of the wire (about a quarter of an inch) bends up into a ninety degree angle at the corner of the hanky which when applied pressure to by the thumb makes the longer piece of the wire rise . By folding the hanky corners in, the tip of the wire rising creates the illusion that a ghost in the hanky is making the center of the handkerchief rise.

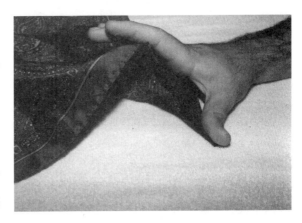

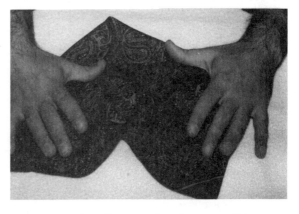

95

The pressure of the thumb on the wire is undetectable and people are preoccupied by the center of the hanky rising to even notice your fingers. I believe that the success of this effect lies in your use of subtlety. I suggest that you get your audience into the mood and have them stare at the hanky for a while (I'm talking a good 15-20 seconds) and then have the hanky move. But have the hanky move only slightly so that the movement is practically unnoticed. This will cause your audience to pay closer attention to the effect. Let the hanky rise a little more and more each time. Between rises, move you hands over the hanky to create the effect that you are pushing the ghost back into the handkerchief.

This effect can be made by getting some material, some thin hard wire, and sewing it yourself, but I suggest that people buy this one at your local shop because the cost is typically pretty cheap and worth avoiding the hassle of making one.

3. The Talking Key

Effect: Dropping a key into a narrow drinking glass or a wide-mouthed bottle, the performer calls upon the spooks to answer questions by causing the key to strike the answers.

A system can be decided upon, such as one clink for "Yes" and two for "No." Immediately, the ghosts go to work. As he holds the glass in his outstretched hand, the key lifts itself and delivers the required strokes. The spooks can make the key count up to numbers as an additional service. The glass can be rested on the table while the clinks occur. Afterward, glass and key may be given for inspection.

96

Method: A heavy glass, a light key, and a loop of thin black thread are the only requirements. The thread is put through the hole in the key; then each end of the thread is wound around a vest button. The key may be carried handily in the vest pocket, as the loop of thread should be more than a foot in length. Experiment will determine the precise measurement most satisfactory.

The key is dropped in the glass, which is taken in one hand. This hand is advanced until the thread is taut. Then, the slightest forward motion of the hand, or withdrawal of the body, will cause the key to lift. An immediate reversal of the motion and the key will fall, accounting for clinks.

In moving from person to person as he carries the glass or sets it down, the performer finds an opportunity to make a slight turn when he is ready to conclude the trick. At this point, the free hand secretly snaps one end of the thread. Setting the glass on a table or handing it to a spectator, the performer promptly walks away, the thread running through the hole in the key and traveling along with him.

Breaking the other end of the thread, the performer lets it fall unnoticed to the floor and no evidence remains to reveal the mystery.

Today, the black thread has been replaced by invisible thread which is so fine it can be used right before your eyes and you will not be able to detect its presence. This invisible thread is available from your favorite magic dealer.

4. The Spooky Weights

Effect: This is perhaps, the most remarkable of pretended psychic effects, well worth the experimentation and practice that are required to accomplish it.

The appliances are simple: a row of empty bottles, all with corks. Through those corks pass cords which dangle down into the bottles, each with a fish-weight on the end. Each bottle has a single cord and weight, given the appearance of a pendulum. Gathering a group about the table, the performer places his hands upon the edge and asks every one to concentrate upon the weights. The performer is seeking to have unseen forces swing the weights—whether they are forces from another sphere or the power of thought coming from the people present.

Soon the spooky pendulums begin to sway—first one, then another. They gradually halt when required and in other ways obey the command of the performer. Yet all the while, the hanging weights are isolated from all contact.

Method: What does it is a slight motion of the table. This is applied by the performer through pressure of his hands. By pressing and relaxing, the weights can be caused to swing and be otherwise controlled. This can become a subconscious action on the performer's part; all he has to do is keep watching the weights and wanting them to move. Those that vary in size will respond to a different tempo. This allows the performer to let people choose the weights that they would prefer to have swing.

Some performers have built up experiments of this type into amazing demonstrations. For general entertainment, however, and particularly with a small group, a single bottle will provide an uncanny enough effect in connection with other spook tricks.

There is a strictly impromptu trick that has points of similarity to the "Spooky Weights." Tie a heavy finger ring or some sort of charm to the end of a thin cord more than a foot in length. Wrap the free end of the cord around your forefinger and thus hold the ring suspended. At command, you can cause the ring to swing sideways, back and forth, or in a circle, halting before each change of direction. It's done by the same system, the unconscious muscular motion of the hand, and therefore it is good practice in connection with the bottle and pendulum. All you have to do is will the ring to act and it will obey. Do not try to force its motions or your hand will visibly jog. By holding the ring above a drinking glass and watching the glass rim, you gain a mental target that causes the ring to sweep in a much larger circle, without conscious control on your part.

An added feature in this impromptu version of the "Spooky Weight" is that you can let other people try it and they will gain the same results, much to their amazement.

97

5. The Floating Table

Effect: The pastime of "table tilting" has often been regarded as something supernormal by persons who have indulged in it. Even today, there are people who believe that it depends upon spirit aid. A group sits about a table, all pressing hands upon the surface. Soon the table begins to tilt, stopping on the count of numbers or during the spelling of names. It may even jounce about the room, driving some of the sitter's from their chairs.

All this is due to the unconscious action of persons in the group. Once enough pressure has been applied to start the table teetering, a lot of action may occur. The irregular pressure of different individuals is a special factor. It is accountable for occasions when the table indulges in surprisingly eccentric behavior. Yet wild gyrations will not convince the skeptic; unless he sees the table actually rise from the floor against the pressure of the hands, he cannot accept the table's actions as anything too extraordinary.

At times, table sitters have reported that the table actually left the floor, though briefly. This is because one person, then another, have exclaimed that the table is actually floating. Coming from opposite sides of the table, this would seem to be corroborative evidence, whereas the time between the reports—a second or less—is the accountable factor, since a tilt has intervened between. A rotary tilt can cause people all around the table to claim it is in midair. Even when persons on opposite sides give such evidence simultaneously, it proves nothing except that the second person was quicker to call out than the first.

To be convincing, the "Floating Table" should occur during a period of comparative calm, rather than in the excitement of a tilting session. This is where the work of the magician enters. Just to show that tables can float by natural means, he demonstrates it to the satisfaction of his audience.

Method: Two methods are herewith described, each requiring a confederate on the side of the table opposite the magician. The first is a brief, impromptu version. Explaining that all persons present must acquire an equal tension, the magician tells them to place their right hands only on the table, the palms flat near the table edge. Next, each person is told to grip his right wrist firmly with his left hand, palm below, thumb and fingers gripping above. The right hands should rest lightly on the table and keep steady.

Suddenly the table rises in uncanny fashion, then descends to the floor. The reason: The magician and his confederate have secretly extended their left forefingers under the right palm and therefore beneath the edge of the table. In this

98

way, they clamp the table between left forefinger and right hand, readily supplying the lift. Amid the amazement, no one will notice that the magician and the other person are showing only three left fingers each, at the side of the right wrist.

This is simply a modification of the more impressive professional system, which was used by spook fakers until magicians took it over for purposes of entertainment. In this version, all hands are laid upon the table. The magician and his confederate each have a special device strapped to a forearm, hidden beneath the sleeve. This appliance consists of a hollow tube containing a plunger or extension rod.

The other hand secretly draws the rod from its tube, just prior to the placement of the hands upon the table. Hidden by the bands beneath which they extend, the rods become the clamps that enable the table to be lifted. Afterward, these plungers are slipped back into the concealed tubes. Sometimes the performer uses two confederates, so that he can call attention to his own hands throughout the demonstration. Here, the confederates are placed directly opposite each other with the rest of the group between.

6. The Spirit Post

Effect: This is a device whereby spooky manifestations can be produced by a performer under conditions which make it seemingly impossible for him to operate. A square post, measuring about four by four inches is set upright on the stage, where it stands about four feet high.

One of the performer's wrists is tied with the end of a rope which can be wired to prevent tampering with the knots. The loose end of the rope is pushed through a hole drilled near the top of the post. The performer's other wrist is then tied and wired with the free end of the rope.

The post is already fixed with angle irons, but to steady it further, a guideline is stapled to the stage, run across the top of the post and stapled on the other side. This line is looped on top of the post and a large spike is driven down into the post to secure the guy-line.

Despite these precautions, the moment the performer is covered with a cabinet, tambourines jangle, bells and horns are blown. All these trappings are in the cabinet with the performer, yet there is no way he could reach them. Any time the cabinet curtain is opened, the performer is seen standing behind the post as firmly tied as ever. Yet the manifestations resume the moment the cabinet is closed again. At the finish, the rope is cut and the performer can show his wrists, still securely bound.

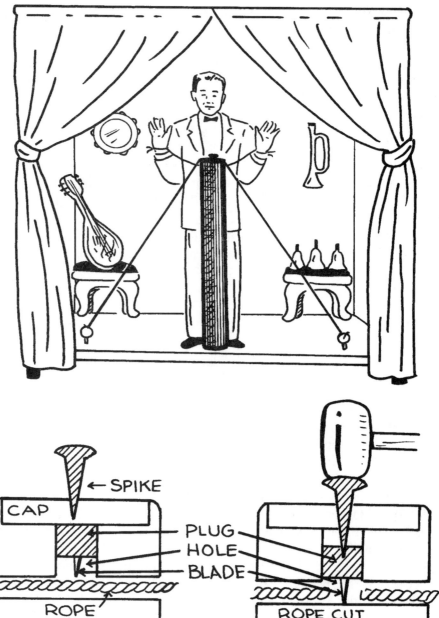

The Spirit Post

Method: As surefire as it is ingenious, this trick depends upon a special construction of the post. Previously, a hole is drilled down through the top of the post to meet the horizontal hole through which the rope is thrust during the binding of the performer's wrists. The vertical hole is fitted with a wooden plug, which has a short, sharp chisel-blade projecting from its lower side. The top of the post is then capped with a block of wood.

The spike used to secure the guideline is not long enough to reach the horizontal hole through which the rope runs. To avoid suspicion of this, the spike is purposely a short one. But after a few strokes from the hammer the spike is driven through the block that caps the post; encountering the concealed wooden plug, the spike forces it downward when the next strokes are made. The chisel-blade is set at right angles to the rope that connects the performer's wrists; hence the blade promptly severs the rope.

The performer is freed to produce manifestations when the cabinet is closed. Afterward, he must keep up the pretence that his wrists are held together, while the rope is cut at each side of the post to release him from what seem to be untampered bonds. Between manifestations, he pushes the severed ropes back into the hole, thus giving an appearance of bondage every time the cabinet curtain opens.

This act was presented in sensational style by a famous British magician, Doctor Lynn.

101

(7. Seance in the Lights)

Effect: Unlike many spook tricks which were originally used by fake mediums and later adapted by magicians, the "Full Light Seance" was first introduced as a strictly magical effect. Its results were probably quite discouraging to the spook fakers, since it made their "dark seances" seem unnecessary.

However, the trick was soon adapted to comedy acts in which the audience was let in on the secret to gain a laugh at the finish. To gain a really spooky effect, it should be done with slightly lowered lights and included with a routine of so-called "manifestations."

Disdaining the use of a cabinet to encourage ghosts, the performer sets bells, tambourines, slates and other equipment on an ordinary table. He takes a large, thick cloth, unrolls it and holds it in front of the table. The performer is standing at the left of the table, his left hand gripping one top corner of the cloth at his right shoulder. His right arm extends behind the cloth, so that his right hand appears at the far corner of the top, stretching the cloth taut.

Immediately, things happen. Bells ring, tambourines beat. The slate pokes itself above the top of the cloth, bearing a written message in answer to a question from the audience. Later, that message is eradicated and another appears instead. Meanwhile, however, the spooks really cavort. Not merely content with making noise, they fling the bells and tambourines over the cloth. Anticipating this, the performer has provided an extra supply at the start. Nevertheless, when the cloth is rolled up, no sign remains of the mysterious spooks.

Method: The cloth used in this trick has a rod running along its upper edge, within the border of the cloth. Affixed to the far corner is an imitation hand, or rather, a portion of one, representing the performer's gripping fingers. When the cloth is unrolled, this dummy comes in sight, the performer keeping his real hand hidden behind the cloth. Working with that hand, the performer manipulates and throws the bells and tambourines, also writing messages, lifting the slate, later erasing it.

Twisting the top of the cloth backward at the finish, the performer promptly brings up his hidden hand and completes the rolling of the cloth in reverse fashion, the dummy fingers going within its fold.

This spooky demonstration was introduced by Carl Germaine, a famous magician of the Chautauqua and Lyceum stages. Germaine presented it in a highly mysterious fashion, giving it the touch of incredibility treat should accompany a spirit seance. Later it was turned into a comedy act by Frank Van Hoven, the "Dippy, Mad Magician" whose vaudeville act was a burlesque of magic in which he purposely bungled many tricks.

This spirit or seance cloth has many uses. It is available in many different qualities and prices.

8. The Hand of Cagliastro

Effect: This spooky trophy is introduced as a replica of the hand of Cagliostro, Master of the Occult, but in magician's parlance it is termed a "Rapping Hand." As such, it derives from a device once used in alleged spirit seances, as the replica is supposedly controlled by the long-departed owner of the original hand.

The hand is made of wood and may be examined by the audience. It is placed on a square sheet of glass, which the performer holds by the sides so that the hand is completely isolated. Then, at the request of the audience and the urge of the performer, the hand begins to rap, bringing its fingers down upon the glass with a sharp clack.

Various questions are answered by the hand. It can rap out ages, usually by tens and units. It raps once for "Yes" and twice for "No." At the finish of the actor seance, the hand and the sheet of glass may both be left with the audience, but no one except the performer can cause it to rap.

Method: This mystery depends upon a peculiar construction of the hand. It is made with straight-carved fingers and the hand itself is tilted at an upward angle in relation to the portion of the wrist attached to it. Because of its shape, the hand—with the wrist—is actually a sort of V-shaped balance that teeters on the base of the thumb and the other side of the hand, near the heel.

HAND TEETERS

The hand is hollow and contains a lead weight. The balance is slightly toward the wrist, so when the hand is set level on the glass, it rests back on the wrist. But the slightest forward tilt of the hand will cause it to teeter forward, bringing the fingers down forcibly against the glass. Its tendency then is to teeter back, so with a little practice the performer can keep the hand rapping in sequence. To finish a series of raps, the glass is tilted back just enough to halt the hand when it returns to its original position, resting on the wrist.

By moving about among his audience, the performer minimizes the slight motion that controls the teetering hand, so that it passes notice. He may also hold the hand at the level of his head resting it on his outspread fingers, as if balancing a tray. This position causes the slight tilting motion of the performer's hand to appear quite natural and it is not connected with the mysterious rapping of the artificial band upon the glass.

Effective though this presentation can prove, the method would be detected by anyone who attempted it, as such a person would learn by experiment that the hand was balanced. To prevent this, the hand is equipped with a sliding weight. Pressure on a knob located at the site of the wrist pushes back an interior rod, so that the weight slides back from the hand into the wrist, where it locks in place. This knob, or plunger, is under a velvet band that girds the wrist.

When he lifts the hand from the glass, the performer holds it with the fingers upward, presses the plunger and then gives the hand for inspection with the glass. Anyone who thinks that tilting is the solution, is due for disappointment upon attempting it. The fingers stay upward and the hand simply slides forward from the glass. To start the hand rapping again, the performer holds it with the fingers pointing down and presses the plunger to send the weight into the hand.

103

104

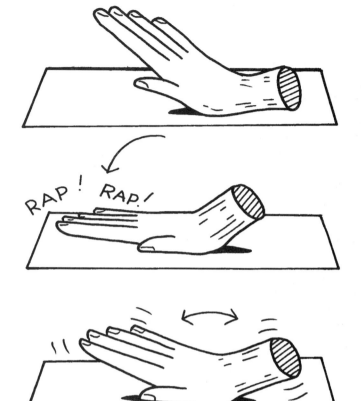

HAND TEETERS

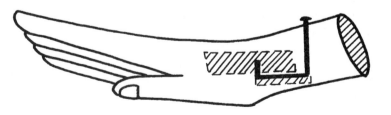

The Hand of Cagliastro

9. Cassadaga Propaganda

Effect: This title was used by the Great Kellar to describe a miniature spirit cabinet which was a feature of his show. It was probably coined as a satirical reference to the Spiritualistic colony at Cassadaga, Now York, as though Kellar were promulgating some of the marvels reputed to occur there.

In contrast to huge cabinets and blackened stages which have been used to produce "spook" effects, this miniature cabinet stands out as quite remarkable. Practically every manifestation short of a human-sized "materialization" can be produced within its limited confines. Moreover, it can be worked on a well-lighted stage, under conditions that make the manifestations seem ghostly indeed.

The "Cassadaga" cabinet is about the size of a large cedar chest or a fair-sized trunk, but is of light construction, with a curtained front. It is standing on the stage and in order to isolate it, the magician lays a sheet of glass across the backs of two chairs. He lifts the cabinet, sets it on the glass and shows the audience various objects such as tambourines, bells and slates. The curtains are opened and these articles are placed within the cabinet, after which the curtains are closed.

Manifestations soon begin. The bells ring, the tambourines jangle, writing appears upon the slates. Various objects are tossed out through the open top of the cabinet. Always, when the performer whisks the curtains open, the cabinet is seen to be quite empty. The extent of the phenomena depends entirely upon the amount of time that the performer devotes to this uncanny mystery, which in Kellar's presentation, left the audience in a very creepy state.

Method: Though basically simple, this miniature cabinet has some ingenious points. The manifestations depend upon a person concealed in the cabinet. This explanation seems nullified by the fact that the cabinet is too small to contain one of the magician's assistants. Actually, however, the concealed operator is a small boy, who requires so much less space that his presence is not suspected.

The chairs and the sheet of glass subtly convey the impression that they could not support much weight, whereas the opposite is the case. When the magician lifts the cabinet and sets it lightly on the glass, all doubt regarding a possible occupant is dispelled. This lift, however, is accomplished by the aid of two thin wires attached to the cabinet. These wires, unseen in the slightly dimmed light, run over pulleys above the stage and have counterbalances that neutralize the boy's weight.

The boy goes out through the back of the cabinet, which is hinged for such a purpose, and takes his position on a small shelf. The curtains may be opened to show the cabinet empty. As soon as the tambourines and bells are in the cabinet, with the curtains closed, the boy takes his cue and reaches inside the cabinet to operate the spirit implements.

At intervals, the cabinet may be shown empty and objects replaced within it, only to have the manifestations repeat themselves.

This trick is rarely performed today.

10. The Knotty Spooks

Effect: Coiling a length of rope, the performer drops it in a box or small spirit cabinet. He leaves one end of the rope projecting from the top. After a friendly spook has had time to do its work, the performer draws out the rope and the audience is amazed to see a series of knots running its entire length. Since the performer couldn't have tied the knots, presumably his pet spook was responsible.

Method: Actually, the performer ties the knots in the process of the coiling, hence this can be shown as a neat impromptu trick as well as a feature of a spook act. Hold the rope across the palms of both hands, which are palms upward. The rope should be more than a yard in length, but only a few inches dangle from the left side of the left hand, the thumb retaining the rope in position.

The right hand is fairly close to the left, the bulk of the rope hanging over the right side of the right hand, retained by the thumb. The right fingers are bent inward. Then the right hand turns inward and downward to the left until its knuckles are toward the left hand. This forms a reverse loop in the rope, which is placed over the left fingers by the right hand. Moving along the rope to the right, the right hand carries another such coil to the left and continues this process until a series of loose coils gird the left fingers. At the finish, the right fingers reach through the coils and draw the left end of the rope through and out at the right. This end is retained when the coiled rope is dropped into the box.

Later, when the magician draws out the rope by that end, he keeps shaking slightly and the knots automatically form themselves, coming into sight one by one.

For stage work, this effect can be accomplished in convincing style on a highly elaborate scale. Two members of a committee are bound with a long rope, each having an end tied around his waist, the knots even being sealed. The rope, twenty feet or more in length, is so long that to bring the two men close together it must be arranged in coils between them. This is particularly true if the pair are to be confined in a spirit cabinet, but it is logical enough on the open stage, if a blackout is to follow.

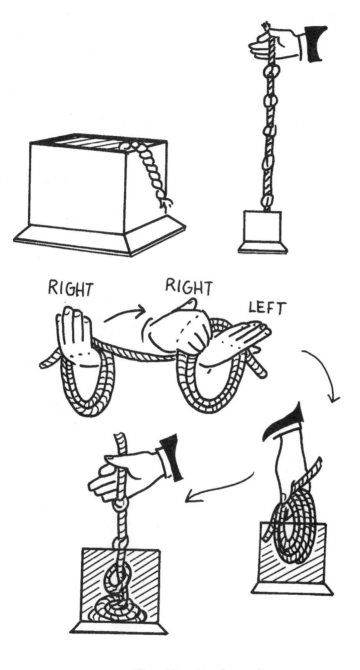

RIGHT

RIGHT

LEFT

The Knotty Spooks

After a comparatively few seconds, the men either step from the cabinet or the lights are turned on. As they walk away from each other, a line of knots is seen in the big rope, apparently tied by the knotty spook.

Though the secret is the same as that of the lesser version, it has a puzzling factor; namely, that the coils are not formed until after the ends of the rope have been tied to the committee men. Hence the rope cannot be manipulated by the performer, as it is too unwieldy for such handling.

The trick depends upon one committee man, who is either a confederate or is taken into confidence when he arrives on the stage. As soon as he is in the dark, this man steps into the center of the rope and lifts all of its coils at once, tip over his head and arms. Stepping away he drops the coils on the stage again. When the two men move apart in the light, knots form in the rope in the usual fashion.

11. Message Reading

Effect: Basic among feats of mentalism is that of "Message Reading" in which the mental wizard answers questions that have been written by members of his audience. The simplest and most direct process is to have such questions folded and dropped into a hat or basket. From this receptacle the performer plucks them one by one, holds them to his forehead and gets reasonably correct "impressions" which he answers.

The time-honored system of performing this mystery is called the "One Ahead," a highly descriptive term which practically reveals the method. The performer holds one question to his forehead, gets only a vague impression. He opens the paper, finds that its question is illegible or unimportant, so he lays it aside. Taking another slip, he gets a definite impression, gives the answer, then opens the paper and reads the question aloud to show how accurate he was.

Method: Actually, the performer merely bluffs with the first paper. Upon opening it, he reads the question written on it, but only to himself. He pretends that the question was trivial or too scrawly to read, because he is actually saving the question for the next slip that he draws from the hat. That's why he answers the second question so well. When he opens the second slip, he reads off the question that was really on the first. Meanwhile he is memorizing a fresh question which he can answer when he holds the third slip to his forehead.

This stunt is very hard to beat. It was a favorite years ago with fake "psychics" and "fortune-tellers," and the small-timers in such trade still use it extensively.

Magicians often neglect it as too elementary, partly on the assumption that keen members of the audience may catch on to the process. Actually it is extremely convincing when sold in serious style by the charlatans who demonstrate it regularly.

When working at a table, the performer simply places each opened question beside the hat or basket. When pretending to read the next question after opening it, he reads from the one that is lying before him. By having a confederate in the audience, the performer can make the first answer a real convincer by addressing his comments to the stooge, who of course corroborates everything the performer says. With a large audience, such a confederate does not put a question in the hat at all. With a small group, he should mark the outside of his paper or fold it in a peculiar style so that the performer can pass it up until it is the last slip in the hat.

This "One Ahead" system can be applied to questions that are sealed in envelopes. In this case, the performer opens each envelope, takes out the question and pretends to read it aloud, as usual reading the one just ahead. Done as an impromptu trick, particularly among friends, this form of "Message Reading" should be done rapidly and with humorous answers. The routine should also be cut short rather than risk too many speculative comments from the audience who are likely to be skeptical as to the mind reader's powers.

This illusion, made famous by talk show host Johnny Carson, is a really cute effect.

109

12. Single Message

Effect: Very effective is the trick of reading a sealed message written by a member of the audience, then handing him the envelope and letting him open it for himself. This is particularly strong when it can be repeated, as is the case in this method. In fact, the several envelopes which are passed around can even be initialed by the spectators, precluding all possibility of substitution.

One precaution is important. The slips of paper given out with the envelopes should be cut to a size slightly smaller than the envelopes themselves. People are told to write questions on the papers, tuck them into the envelopes without bothering to fold them. Otherwise—though he doesn't mention it—the performer will encounter complications.

Method: The performer has a large stack of envelopes from which he distributes some in which the spectators can peace their written slips. Only about half of the envelopes are genuine. The rest are glued to form a dummy stack. Not only that, the stack is hollowed out and inside it is a flashlight of the square type which resembles a miniature electric lantern. In working this trick today you can obtain a small flashlight that will light when you squeeze it. Either that, or the flashlight is rigged specially to fit inside the dummy stack.

Lying flat in the stack, the flashlight has its bulb in the center, pointing upward. As a precaution against giving this device away, the flashlight may be hidden by a thin strip of paper pasted across the opening above it. The bottom of the dummy stack is of course firm and solid, being reinforced with cardboard like a box.

The envelopes should not be very large as the purpose is to reveal their contents in X-ray fashion by using the gleam of the flashlight. This is done as follows: In gathering the real envelopes, the performer places them on the bottom of the stack, holding the stack upside down so the bottom looks like the top. The real envelopes go below the dummy. Drawing one envelope off and holding it to his forehead, the performer lets his hand turn over with the stack.

Now, when the envelope is brought away from the forehead and briefly laid there, it comes just above the hidden flashlight. Keeping the stack turned toward him, the performer presses a concealed switch. The light glows through the envelope, enabling him to read the writing on the paper within it.

Drawing away the envelope, the performer gestures with it, holds it to his head again and finally answers the question or reveals whatever words he saw on the paper. He returns the envelope to its owner, unopened. Then he proceeds to read another question in the same fashion. This is continued until the performer has read as many questions as he desires. Sometimes of course he encounters "confused thought impressions" but that is only when he meets with a folded or poorly written slip.

In this trick, it is advisable to have considerable distance between the performer and his audience. Also, the performer should be fairly well surrounded by lights. Such details are essential so as to prevent the spectators from noting any strange glow emanating from the neighborhood of the performer's hand. Fake mediums would attribute that to ectoplasmic phenomena, but we are considering the subject strictly in terms of magical entertainment.

There is a version of this effect called *The Thought Transmitter* that is popular in the magic market now. It is a bit pricey but well worth it if you're performing regularly. I saw a mentalist perform this trick for an audience of 600 and blow them away.

Single Message

13. The Untouched Card

Effect: When a performer manipulates a pack, it's Magic; when he reveals a card without touching the pack or even seeing a person take a card, it's called Mentalism. All of which adds up to Magic, which is the superlative in all events, whether or not a trick happens to come in what seems a purely mental category. Two packs are used in this trick, or "test," as it is commonly called. The performer hands one to a spectator, has him run through the cards faces up, showing them to the audience. The spectator may also shuffle the pack if he wishes. The performer meanwhile runs through his pack in the same style, displaying a variety of jumbled faces.

Then to make all fair, the performer takes the pack which the spectator shuffled, giving him the other pack in exchange. Placing the pack he has just received face downward in his left hand, the performer tells the spectator to do the same. The magician then states that he wants the spectator to cut somewhere about the middle of the pack, and lifting the upper group, to look squarely at the bottom card of that group. He is to note and remember that one card only, taking care to observe no others. Then he is to replace the upper portion of the pack back on the lower.

The magician illustrates this with his pack so there can be no mistake. At the same time, he restrains the spectator by saying, "Not yet!" Having conveyed to the spectator just what he is to do, the magician sends him to the far corner of the room, so he can note a card while his back is turned. The spectator may step outside the room if a door is handy.

Upon the spectator's return, the performer tells him to lay his pack aside. Not once does the magician intend to touch it. He wants the spectator simply to think of his card and think hard. During that process, the magician runs through the pack that he is holding and finally draws a card from it. He tells the spectator to name his card aloud. This is done and the magician triumphantly shows the drawn card to the entire audience. It is the very card that the spectator named, after noting it in the other pack!

Method: This minor miracle is accomplished very simply. At the start, the magician has a "Forcing Pack" in which a batch of the cards are exactly alike. In the old days, such a deck contained fifty-one identical cards with an odd card for the bottom. This particular pack has only about half its cards identical, but they are sandwiched between two groups of indifferent cards, top and bottom.

While the spectator is running through an ordinary pack, the magician casually does the same with the "Forced Pack." He slides cards openly from left to right until he has displayed about a dozen, then with his left thumb he pushes over the bulk of the cards and continues his slow, emphatic exhibit with the last dozen cards at the top.

This is the pack which the magician plants in the hand of his helper, taking the ordinary pack in exchange. When the obliging volunteer cuts to somewhere near the center, as the performer illustrates, he just can't miss getting one of the "Forcers." When the man returns, the performer has him lay that pack aside. From the ordinary pack, the magician draws out the necessary card and the trick is as good as done. Careful attention to detail and dramatic effect are the elements that build the mystery.

14. Duplicated Thought

Effect: Slates are popular items with the mental worker, as any writing on them appears clearly and can be erased later, like a fleeting thought. Yet there are times when those thoughts are not as fleeting as they might seem. Such is certainly true in this instance of a duplicated idea.

The mentalist passes a slate and a piece of chalk to a spectator, requesting that he hold the slate so that he alone can see its nearer surface. Beside the spectator, the performer places a moistened sponge or cloth. Then, while the performer is a considerable distance away, he asks the person to write any initials, figures or geometric design that he may wish.

During the writing, the performer avoids glancing at the spectator. He suggests that the written item be shown to a few trusted persons for later verification. He asks the writer to concentrate upon the inscription for a period of about a dozen seconds. Then, sure that he has caught the impression, the performer tells the spectator to obliterate the writing with the sponge.

That done, the performer takes the slate, shows it all about, proving that the surface is damp and clean. He lays the slate aside, concentrates a short while and finally takes the chalk and begins to mark something on the slate himself. Finally, the performer asks the spectator to name what he inscribed, that is, the mental image which he still retains. As soon as the description is given, the performer turns the state to the audience.

There, in exact detail, is the performer's reproduction of the very thought which the spectator put in chalk, only to eradicate before the performer could have seen it.

Method: Apparently this demonstration precludes all chance of trickery, particularly where the slate is concerned. Indeed, the value of slate tests lies in the

113

fact that in many instances the slate is comparatively innocent. In this case it is completely so, though it plays a part. The article upon which success hinges, yet which passes totally unsuspected by the audience, is the chalk.

This particular chalk has previously been soaked in oil, which gives a greasy effect to anything it writes. This is so slight that it escapes detection and when the slate is cleaned with a damp cloth, the oil impression is temporarily eliminated against the deep blackness of the slate. Rubbing with a dry cloth would not be sufficient and would have a tendency to smudge. But the water has no effect on the oil, though it does render it unnoticeable for a brief time.

That brief time is the period required for the slate to dry. Therefore, the performer must go through a few attempts at concentration unless he is combining this test with another and is picking up some other person's impression first. When the slate is dry, the performer naturally uses it to register his own thoughts and in the light he sees a thin, dim replica of whatever his victim wrote.

Over this product of the oil slick, the mentalist chalks his own impression which cannot fail to duplicate the original inscription.

Through the years new and improved impression slates have been invented. They are a big improvement over this old method.

114

15. Color Vision

Effect: The magician has a cube with a different color on each side. The magician asks a spectator to secretly choose a color and place the cube in a box so that the chosen color faces the lid of the box.

The spectator puts the lid on and gives the box to the magician. Through extrasensory powers the magician is able to figure out which color was chosen. He tells the audience and then opens the lid to prove he is correct.

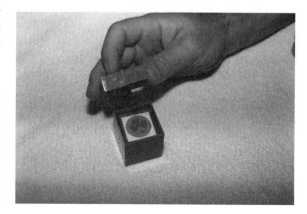

Method: The method is simple. Everything described in the effect actually occurs except the extrasensory part. The magician actually lifts the lid without the audience realizing it and peaks at the color. The easiest method

I've seen to do this is by simply turning your back to the spectator when the volunteer is choosing a color. You can justify this movement by explaining that you don't want anyone to think that you would sneak a peek at the color. Tell the volunteer "After you've chosen a color and placed the lid on the box I'll know your done because you've dropped the box in my hands." Put your hands behind your back as if you're waiting for the box. When they've placed the box in your hands, simply turn around so that your hands and the box are still behind your back and momentarily out of site.

At this moment you should slide the lid off the top of the box and move it to the side. This position allows for you to peak at the color but makes the audience believe that the box is closed the way they left it. The only important part now is to make sure that the audience doesn't see the open side. You also want to be subtle as you peak at the chosen color. One method is to make a dramatic gesture that ends with the box being placed against your forehead so that the

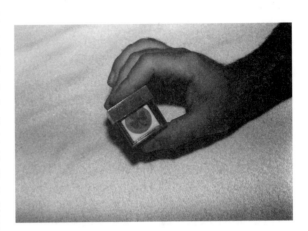

open side is against your skin . If you say "ouch" as the box hits your forehead, you are guaranteed a laugh. People love watching others get hurt.

When you reveal the chosen color, you can create drama and suspense by first eliminating some of the other colors. For example, if the chosen color is blue you might say, "I know that you didn't pick red. And you didn't pick yellow or green. You didn't choose brown either. No, no, I believe (dramatic pause), and sometimes I'm wrong (another dramatic pause), but I think I'm right this time when I say that you've chosen the color... blue." When you finally say blue your audience will go crazy.

Then you have to open the box to show the color without letting your audience see that the lid has moved. To accomplish the you lift the lid

off and simultaneously tilt the box so the opening faces up. The beautiful part of this effect is that you can hand the cube, box, and lid out for inspection and let the audience try this fantastic feat. A good rule to remember is that whenever you can let the audience inspect props they will be pleased. Most magic shops sell this trick under the name *Color Vision*, but if you can't remember the name or if the effect is under a different name, describe the effect to the salesperson and I'm sure they will be able to find it for you. Don't be fooled that it is a cheap effect just because it is inexpensive. A good performance of this trick can make the effect priceless.

16. Magazine Prediction

Effect: The magician shows the audience an envelope and says, "In this envelope I've written on a card a premonition I had earlier. It was a word." The magician hands the envelope to a spectator. Another spectator is brought up to the stage. The spectator is given three magazines and asked to choose one. From the chosen magazine the spectator will choose a word. To prove that the spectator isn't an accomplice the magician blindfolds the spectator so that they won't even know what word they are choosing. The spectator is allowed to open to any page and they are asked to draw an "X" on the page. The words that the two lines of the "X" cross over becomes the chosen word. The blindfold is taken off the spectator and they are instructed to read the word out loud. Then the other spectator holding the prediction is asked to rip open the envelope and read the word on the card inside. Low and behold the premonition was correct because the two volunteers read the same word.

Method: To perform this trick you must actually force the spectator to choose a very specific word – the word you've written down on the card. To do this you must first choose one word from a magazine. I like to choose a descriptive or odd word. Perhaps the word is *lightbulb*. Draw an "X" over the word in the magazine and write down that word on a card. Next thing you need to do is get a dried out pen or marker. You can dry out a marker fairly quickly by taking the cap off of a marker and letting it sit out in the sun. The cheaper the marker, the faster it will dry out. So the "X" is already drawn on the word in the magazine and the spectator thinks they are drawing an "X" but is actually using a dried out marker or pen. Because the spectator is blindfolded they never realize that they are using a dried out marker. It is important to have the spectator close the magazine before they take off their blindfold so they won't realize the page number.

Then the only thing that is left to do is to force the spectator to choose the correct magazine out of three with which they will draw the X in. This is done using the magician's force (Refer to Close-up magic for explanation of magician's force explained in the Effect Four Coins and a Magic Mouth). If you do not want to use the magician's force to get the spectator to choose the correct magazine you can rig three magazines by finding the same word in all three of them.

17. The Marked Name

Effect: Showing a large slate, the performer holds it upright and asks people to call out names at random. These may be simple first names: John, Mary, or whatever anyone may call. They may be names from a group, such as those of presidents or famous men—even cities or countries.

As the names are called, the performer writes them on the slate so that they form a column of some eight or ten names, with a space at the left. Now he asks that a committee decide upon which name is to be used for an experiment in mental concentration. The committee may even retire to another room and attempt to project the thought from there.

In no case is the mentalist to be given any inkling of the name. He faces the audience, holding the name side of the slate toward himself. Running his hand up) and down the slate, he hesitates here and there, finally announcing that he has marked an "X" in front of one of the names.

The committee then is summoned and is told to announce the chosen name. We will suppose that it is "Margy," at position seven in the column. Calmly, the mentalism turns the slate around and shows the "X" at the left of the name Margy, proof absolute that he plucked the thought of the committee through some process of Mental Radio.

Method: Quite convincing, this trick, yet very simple of execution. The trick lies in the slate, which is specially prepared for this. The slate is furnished with a flat square of metal, painted jet black, like the surface of the slate. On this metal tab is an "X" painted in white to resemble a chalk mark.

The metal tab extends from beneath the frame at the left of the slate. The end beneath the frame is fitted in a groove. At the very edge of the slate proper is an upright pin, attached to the tab. All the performer has to do is run his thumb up and down the edge of the slate frame and the metal tab will slide along. The pin is set at the bottom edge of the tab, so the metal square can be pushed out of sight under the top frame of the slate, which is furnished with a slight space to receive it.

117

With the metal tab hidden at the start, the slate is quite ordinary in appearance. After writing the names, the performer goes into his moments of concentration and makes a great show of hesitancy, as though starting to mark an "X" at one spot and then another. He can also pretend to make a mark, then rub it out. All this is to prevent the audience from guessing where he actually puts the "X" mark. As a matter of fact, the performer makes no mark at all. He simply announces that he has done so; then, without showing the name side of the slat, he awaits the verdict of the committee.

When the name is stated, the performer is holding the slate with both hands, his left thumb at the upper left corner, pressing the pin. As he steps forward, he draws his thumb down to the chosen name, bringing the marked tab to the right position. Releasing his right hand, he turns the slate around with his left, showing the "X" in front of the name. Being black against black, the metal tab is never noticed or suspected.

The maneuver is natural and no more than momentary. It is never noticed because of the motion of the slate which the performer can be lowering, then turning, as he is stepping forward. As an added throw-off, the performer can be holding the chalk between the fingers of his right hand, on the near side of the slate. This not only attracts attention; if the name is far down the list, the performer can draw the tab part way, then lay the chalk aside with his right hand. After that, the right hand again grips the slate long enough for the left thumb to complete the adjustment of the tab.

Immediately afterward, the performer rubs out the names with a cloth. During this process he pushes the tab up out of sight beneath the upper frame. Thus when the slate is shown it is entirely blank, the "X" mark apparently having been erased with the names.

This trick has an advantage in that it can be performed as an experiment in thought projection instead of reception, thus fitting with different styles of programs. As a projection test, the mentalist states that he will pick a name and send it mentally to the committee, or preferably to some individual chosen by the audience.

The performer asks the recipient—or receiving group—to announce the name which made the strongest impression. When the name is stated, the mentalist turns the slate around and shows that he marked that very name.

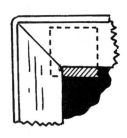

The Marked Name

18. The Random Mind

Effect: Purveyors of mental wizardry are frequently called upon to present some impromptu demonstration of their wares under conditions that will suit the most exacting skeptic. Nothing could be more convincing than letting the skeptic himself choose a total stranger with whom the mentalist is to perform an experiment in telepathy. That is exactly what happens in this case.

While the effect may be presented during a regular performance, it is more suitable for a small group, as in a restaurant, hotel lobby, or anywhere that strangers may be available. Taking a note book and pencil from his pocket, the performer requests the skeptic to pick out some friendly-looking person who might be willing to test out the mental waves. Such a person is invited to join the group and the performer tears off a sheet of note paper, folds it twice and hands it to the stranger along with a pencil.

"I would like you to take this paper some distance away," the performer says. "Then turn your back, unfold the paper and write a number of three figures. Understand, I want a number of three figures to be written on the paper; then fold it and bring it back to me. At no time are you to speak a word to anyone. Is that agreed?"

The friendly stranger nods, goes away with the paper and pencil. Concentrating, the performer writes a number on another sheet of paper, using another pencil. He folds this paper and drops it in a glass or lays it beneath a match pack. The stranger returns and the performer tells him to place his paper in another glass or beneath another match pack. When the skeptic opens the two folded slips, he finds that each bears the identical number.

Method: On the basis of one chance in a thousand, this result seems uncanny, but the performer is dealing with a person, not a number. On the bottom surface of the top sheet of the pad, the performer has previously written a number, say 388. When he folds the paper, he does so in downward fashion. Hence the folded paper that he hands the stranger actually has a number written on it. That number, however, has not been seen by anyone.

When the stranger retires with the folded paper, he opens it intending to write a number. To his surprise, he discovers a number already there and he begins to catch on to the part that he is to play. As an added hint, the performer has given him a pencil without an eraser or a point, so the stranger can neither rub out the number nor inscribe a new one.

Being that far in the game, the stranger's tendency is to play it through. He folds the paper and brings it back. Meanwhile, the performer, disguising his writing, is putting down the number 388 on another sheet of paper, which he folds. Having been told to say nothing, the stranger simply places his paper where told. When it is opened, its number corresponds with that on the performer's sheet.

Bold though it is, this flimflam has just the twist that leads to its success, particularly when demonstrated by a clever operator. In his wording, his request for strict silence, the performer is selling the stranger on the idea from the start. If the stranger has a pencil, the performer may even borrow it, then lend the man his own, which makes it all the more pointed—but not the pencil!

Should the stranger refuse to cooperate or give the thing away, the performer can brush it off as a joke, even stating that he tried it just to prove how difficult it is to influence a person into becoming a confederate. This however is something that will very rarely happen. About the only hazard is that the stranger may not catch on and may prove dumb enough to return, saying a number was already written on the paper.

To avoid that, the performer can have a little typewritten slip, telling the spectator just what he is to do, which includes putting the direction slip in his pocket. Or the slip can tell him what number he is to write, saying that the stunt is just a game on the party. Such a slip is already tucked beneath the top sheet of the note book when the performer tears it off and folds it. But the experienced performer can sell the idea without relying on this added subterfuge.

This clever device has been attributed to the celebrated "Doctor" Reese, who for years convinced his clients that he was a genuine telepathist. The final stage of the game is to thank the stranger and politely get him to bow out of the picture. This is not too difficult, but it is claimed that Reese took no chances on that score. It is said that his system was to fold a dollar bill inside the paper and have the skeptic pick a bellboy or a waiter as the stranger in the test. In accepting and pocketing this tip, the impromptu stooge would find it good policy to remain silent.

121

19. In The Crystal

Effect: Crystal balls are commonly associated with mind reading and clairvoyance. Usually it is the mentalist who gazes into a crystal to learn the answers to questions that his audience has offered. In this case the situation is the opposite and therefore quite astounding. Stating that he will project a mental image of a playing card previously chosen by he audience or selected at random, the performer lets a spectator gaze into a crystal ball and see the answer. Without a word from the mentalist, the spectator names the card, much to the amazement of the audience and sometimes to his own bewilderment.

Method: The secret is simple but effective. The performer has a tiny playing card printed on thin paper. This little slip is moistened and placed on the ball of the thumb. In picking up the crystal, the performer transfers the slip to the glass ball, which should be at least three inches in diameter. He places the crystal in the spectator's hand so that the little card is at one side.

Now, by simply lifting the person's hand, the card comes into sight through the crystal and is not only magnified but appears to be an image within the crystal itself. When the person names the card he saw there, the performer takes the crystal, sliding off the little card with his thumb. In presenting the trick in full, he ether forces a playing card on the audience or pretends to take one at random from the pack. The notion is that by having the entire group concentrate on that card, the man with the crystal will gain its mental image in the ball. If a susceptible person is chosen, he is often more impressed than the remainder of the audience.

20. Calling All Cards

Effect: This begins as an astounding mental mystery and finishes as a comedy stunt; but each depends upon the other, as will be evident from the explanation.

Stating that he will cause any spectator to become a mental marvel, the performer asks the audience to choose the person that they want, specifying only that a man be designated. This done, the performer places the man in a chair facing a corner of the room.

Taking a pack of cards, the performer tells the audience that he will show them one by one and that the man in the corner will catch the thought waves and name the cards. Showing the top card, the performer asks its name and the man says "Three of Hearts" which is correct. Showing the next card, the performer asks its identity and is told "Seven of Spades." This also is correct as are the next cards shown, until the volunteer assistant has named as many as a dozen cards in a row.

Method: This is just the first part of the demonstration, but before proceeding with a description of the sequel, it is advisable to explain the mystery so far.

In placing the spectator in the corner, the performer asks him to rest his hands in front of him. Into the man's hand the performer puts a card which says: Let's work a stunt on the crowd. When I ask you to name cards, call them as follows: Three of Hearts, Seven of Spades, Jack of Diamonds, Four of Clubs, Two of Diamonds, Ace of Spades, Nine of Clubs, Jack of Hearts, King of Spades, Eight of

Clubs, Ace of Diamonds, Queen of Spades. After that, put this list in your pocket and say nothing.

The performer has memorized the list of cards and has them on top of the pack in that order. Invariably the volunteer assistant will enter into the spirit of the thing. As the performer shows the cards and asks their names, the stranger calls them.

That's all there is to it, but it can prove very amazing. However, if the trick ended there, people would ask too many questions, particularly of the stranger. So the performer switches immediately to the comedy sequel.

Stating that he would like to test another thought recipient, the performer asks that a woman be chosen. She is placed in the corner, but is given no list. Shuffling the pack, the performer places his finger to his lips, requesting the audience to preserve silence. He then starts showing cards, asking the woman to name them.

Since the lady is only guessing, she names each card wrong, but every time the performer announces "Correct" and again gestures for the witnesses to remain silent. When he says "That's enough," the woman will immediately exclaim that she simply called each card as it came to mind and is more amazed than anyone else because of the result.

By then, the whole audience will be laughing and the lady will soon catch on to the joke. Afterward, however, people will begin thinking back and wondering how the man who first played "assistant" managed to hit every card as called. As a result, the performer will be credited with having performed a very amazing mental test before lapsing into a bit of humor.

21. Nailed Thoughts

Effect: Announcing that he will present an experiment in sheer telepathy, the performer produces a new, scaled pack of cards and requests that the pack be opened, then shuffled thoroughly by several persons present. The pack is then wrapped in a piece of newspaper and placed upon a board. A nail is driven through the pack and deep into the board.

Turning his back or standing some distance away, the performer tells a person to tear the newspaper and draw cards from the top of the pack, one by one, ripping them from the nail. The person is to look at each card as it comes free and the performer will catch the thoughts instantaneously. This is exactly what happens. One by one, the mental marvel calls off the names of the cards as the person rips them free and notes them.

Method: This is an excellent example of the claptrap that can turn a simple trick into a pseudo-miracle. All that the performer requires is a dozen extra cards to match the new pack that is used. These extras are arranged in an order which the performer memorizes. They are placed in the center of a folded sheet of newspaper. The other half of the paper is then folded over to conceal the cards and a few dabs of paste or wax are applied outside the corners of the cards to keep them in position. The doubled paper is then creased, close to the edges of the hidden cards.

After a new pack has been opened and thoroughly shuffled by different persons, the performer asks someone to look through it and remove the joker or any advertising cards. The joker is laid face down on the table; then the pack is given another shuffle and is placed face down on the joker. The performer introduces the sheet of newspaper, holds it on his hand and asks that the pack be laid in the center, face up, the joker preventing anyone from seeing the other cards in the pack. The pack is then folded in the paper, which is turned over, placed on the board and the nail driven through.

Now, when the paper is torn and the top cards ripped from the nail one by one, the cards actually come from the special packet between the double layer of paper. The performer calls them off in order, stopping the process before the group is exhausted, so that the person does not reach the layer of paper separating the group from the actual pack. Since the pack is now useless, the performer tosses it aside, board and all, along with the ripped cards. This disposal is natural and no one ever thinks of examining the mutilated cards as a clue to the mystery.

The performer must be sure to hold the prepared paper so that its concealed cards are face upward when the pack is placed thereon. Adherence to this precaution avoids about the only pitfall that might be encountered. Of course a pack of cards is ruined, but the result is worth it.

A bolder method of adding the extra cards is to have them in the coat pocket. After the pack has been repeatedly shuffled, the performer palms the extras from his pocket. Receiving the pack with his free hand, he squares it, face down, adding the extra cards, and promptly sets it on an ordinary sheet of newspaper so that the pack can be wrapped and nailed to the board. In the hands of a skilled worker, this is never detected. New packs of cards are always less bulky than those which have been used; hence the addition of a dozen more cards does not make the pack look too thick.

22. Nine Out of Nine

Effect: Though more of an impromptu effect than a deep-dyed mental mystery, this can be used with a committee, with very good results. It also has advantages as a "preliminary test" to learn if a person is in the "mental mood" for a serious telepathic experiment.

The subject is given a sealed envelope, which he is told contains some cards. He is then asked to write a number, containing as many figures as he wishes: three, four, five, or even more. This may be written on the envelope or a pad of paper. He is then told to reverse the number, figure for figure and to subtract the smaller from the larger.

For example: The person writes 38224. Reversed, this is 42283. Subtracting 38224 from 42283 leaves 4059. But the process does not stop there. The person is told to add the figures in the remainder, which he does. In this case, they would total 18. He is told that if the total comes to more than I 0 (which in this case it does) he is to add the figures again. In this instance, I and 8 will give him 9.

None of this calculation is noted by the performer but it may be checked by another spectator. The performer then hands the subject four tiny boxes, asks him to take his choice, open the box, and note the color of a tiny block or wad of paper that he finds inside. The subject does this and finds—for example—a red block.

Opening the large envelope, the performer shows that it contains a batch of blank cards of different colors, such as red, yellow, green, and blue. Running through those cards, the performer shows that the reds predominate, numbering more than all the rest together. In fact, the red cards representing the chosen color—total exactly nine, which was the lone figure that came from the elaborate calculation.

People aren't always willing to accept this even as a coincidence. They have a habit of looking into the other boxes to find out if they contain red blocks too. But they do not. The remaining boxes contain blocks of yellow, green and blue respectively, and the result is a real mystery.

Method: Inasmuch as the properties used in this trick are easily obtained, a careful study of the details will enable the reader to try it out at very short notice. If it sounds complicated at first reading, remember that its complexities are all planned as part of the game, which is to confuse the spectators. Actually, it all cracks down to a simple process.

The number nine is the key. Any number of several figures, reversed, with a subtraction following, will give a number whose figures add up to a multiple of nine (such as 9, 18, 27). Where two figure numbers are concerned, they will reduce to nine when the figures are added. So the performer is sure of that part.

Now for the matter of the cards. There are exactly twelve cards. Nine of them are reds, so if red proves to be the chosen color, the performer has only to open the envelope, spread out the cards and show that there are exactly nine red cards, though each of the other colors is represented only by a single card.

The ninth card from the top of the packet, however, is the green card. So if green should be the chosen color, the performer says nothing about the total number of red cards. Instead, he counts off the cards one by one and shows that the ninth from the top is a green card, the only green one in the lot.

Fourth from the top of the packet is the blue card. If blue happens to be the chosen color, the performer simply turns over the envelope before he opens it. Thus when he counts down to nine, the blue card is the one that turns up at that number.

This leaves only the yellow card to be considered. It is the top card of the packet. On its under side is written the word "Nine" in bold letters. In the previous examples, in weeding out nine red cards or counting down nine to the green card, the cards are not turned over. Hence no one realizes that there is anything written on the yellow card. In the case of blue, the count ends before the performer reaches the yellow card; but after showing the blue card at position nine, he should absently turn over the three remaining cards before spreading them to show there is no blue among them. Again, the writing on the yellow card will remain unrevealed.

Should yellow be chosen, however, the performer first turns over the envelope. He then removes the cards and shuffles them before spreading them out. Somewhere in the batch, the yellow card will show up, hearing its bold message of "Nine."

This trick would be a good one if it worked nine times out of ten. It does better than that; it works nine out of nine. No need to worry about the tenth time—it can't happen.

23. Relayed Thought

Effect: Most performers of mental magic enliven their routine by using some unusual methods of revealing the thoughts that they have garnered from the audience. Inasmuch as the mentalist does experiments in thought projection as well as reception, it is logical that he should be able to convey one person's thought to another, with the performer himself acting solely as a relay.

126

Method: The method about to be described serves that purpose, though it may be reduced if desired to an experiment in straight thought projection, as that is the part in which the trick device is used. However, the combination is more effective, so "Relayed Thought" will be given in its entirety.

Some gentleman in the audience having noted the serial number of a dollar bill, or taken a card from a pack, the performer extends a short rope and asks that the gentleman take one end of it, the performer holding the other end in his left hand. Taking another length of rope, the performer retains one end in his right hand and asks a lady to hold the loose end.

Now the performer asks the gentleman to concentrate upon the first figure of the bill, which he may be holding in his free hand. As the performer counts steadily from one to nine, adding zero if necessary, the gentleman is to give a mental command of "Stop" when the right figure is reached. The lady is instructed to stay "Stop" aloud, should she gain any impression or impulse at the announcement of a certain number.

As the performer counts, the lady suddenly says, "Stop"—at the number five, for example—and the gentleman nods that it is the figure on which he concentrated. This is repeated again and again, the lady stopping the count on every figure of the dollar bill's number. Sometimes the performer goes through the entire count, telling the lady to name the impulse number when he finishes. The result in this case will be the same. Similarly, the performer can call off the name of a playing card, first by suit and then by value, and the lady will get the mental impression.

If a dollar bill is used, the performer simply borrows one from the audience and switches it for a bill of his own—the number of which he has memorized—before handing it to the man who is to work in this experiment. In a case of a playing card, it is forced on the gentleman, who is serving only as a blind, since he really has no part in the trick.

The lady is therefore the important factor. On that account, the performer gives her the end of a special rope. This rope is a casing over a rubber tube that has a bulb at one end, a tiny bag of thin rubber at the other. The bulb is hidden in the performer's hand; the "palpitator," as the thin bag is termed, is in the rope itself, at the end which the lady holds.

When the performer secretly squeezes the bulb, the palpitator expands and supplies a slight, mysterious pressure within the lady's hand. Accepting this as the expected impulse, she halts the count at that point, or remembers that particular number. Having no idea of the cause, she supposes it to have something to do with a mental impression.

Information gained from a scaled message—such as the month, day, and year of a birth—can also be relayed in this fashion.

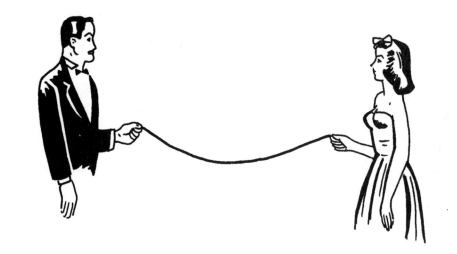

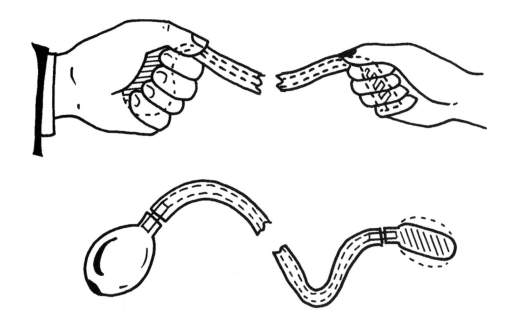

Relayed Thought

Part 5
Grand Illusion

The spectacular period of magic began shortly before the present century with the introduction of the great stage shows which have continued ever since. At that time, the leading magician in America was Alexander Herrmann, styled Herrmann the Great, an amazing wizard of Mephistophelean appearance who toured the country in his private railroad car, carrying a company of assistants and tons of baggage.

It was Herrmann who first emphasized the large-scale art of the illusionist in contrast to the ordinary style of stage magic, the distinction being that stage illusions consist of magic performed with living people or huge objects, rather than small or inanimate objects. Herrmann vanished ladies, floated them in air, and even produced a huge array of animals from an empty Noah's Ark that took up a goodly proportion of the stage.

When Herrmann died suddenly in 1896, he was succeeded by his nephew Leon, who adopted the title of Herrmann the Great and copied his uncle's style and makeup for a decade. Later a nephew by marriage styled himself Felix Herrmann and carried some of the Herrmann tradition clear into the 1930's. This explains why many people today claim to have once seen "Herrmann" though the original Great died before their time.

Herrmann's greatest rival was Harry Kellar, who became America's leading illusionist until 1909 when he announced Howard Thurston as his successor. Thurston enlarged the show far beyond the size of Kellar's and toured for more than twenty years with a full evening performance, frequently introducing new illusions or reviving old ones.

During those years, many other magicians were rising to fame as illusionists, mostly in the vaudeville field. Among them was Harry Blackstone, who by 1940 had the largest magic show on tour in America and presented full evening performances in cities from coast to coast, throughout the entire theatrical season, thus establishing himself as the fourth in the great line of Herrmann, Kellar and Thurston.

In their search for the spectacular, the great magicians began producing entire choruses of girls from a single empty cabinet. They vanished horses, automobiles and even elephants. Not content with merely levitating ladies, they vanished them while they were in midair. One vaudeville magician even made a specialty of floating a piano and the player with it. In the course of things, they introduced new styles of illusions in which girls were sawed, spiked, crushed, and even burned alive, all without the slightest harm.

Among the vaudeville illusionists whose elaborate presentations ranked them with full evening performers was the Great Leon, who condensed much of a two-hour show into thirty minutes. Another headliner was George LaFollette, who often appeared twice on a bill first as LaFollette, a quick-change-artist, then as Rush Ling Toy in an act of Chinese magic and illusions. Few persons realized that the two performers were one and the same.

This case of dual identity brought LaFollette special mention in Ripley's "Believe It or Not" and it is approached only by the instance of Chung Ling Soo, to be mentioned later in this chapter. But LaFollette, when he appeared as Rush Ling Toy, carried his double personality on to the stage itself, something probably unparalleled in the annals of magic. He still performs in both guises, though the public has now been acquainted with the fact.

To draw comparisons between the magical greats of the American stage would be difficult, not because they reached their peaks at different periods, but because of the individual characteristics that contributed to their greatness. Herrmann was noted for the air of mystery that surrounded his performances. Kellar reputedly could baffle even magicians, time and again, with certain of his tricks. Thurston's forte was the dramatic, which he carried to great intensity. Blackstone stands as inimitable in his ability to carry his work before the curtain and hold an audience spellbound with his smaller magic after the climax of a great illusion.

Only a real master of the magic art can stand the test of a full evening show over long, continued seasons. This does not in any way disparage the fine work of magicians in lesser fields, some of whom undoubtedly could have gained the highest rating if given opportunity or inclination. But the art of magic is judged by its greats and it stands by their achievements. That fact offers a basis of comparison between the famous magicians of the American stage and the great American magicians whose fame was gained elsewhere. Most celebrated of the latter was Maurice Raymond, who circled the world seven times, carrying as many as three complete evening shows in order to play extended engagements in the capital cities of many lands. Known as the Great

130

Raymond, he gave complete performances in nine different languages, which accounted for his popularity in the countries where he appeared during a career of more than fifty years. Raymond's friend Elbert Hubbard termed him the "King of America" in recognition of the worldwide charm of his magic and his personality.

Another American magician who presented large-scale magic on a global basis was Charles Carter, who gained much of his fame in the Orient, but seldom performed in America. In later years, Dante presented a huge magic show in South America and Europe, returning to New York just before the war. There he presented his show on Broadway and followed with an American tour. Less fortunate was the Great Nicola, whose last world tour was interrupted at Singapore, where his equipment sank with a ship that struck a mine.

On the list of the much-traveled greats was Carl Rosini, who gained fame as a vaudeville illusionist in the United States, then carried his magic through South America to win an equal reputation there. Rosini has toured other lands as well and has made a specialty of presenting Oriental mysteries before American audiences. Among the noted American magicians to visit India was Jack Gwynne, who offered huge rewards to any fakirs who could show him the mythical Rope Trick, but found no takers.

Among the Oriental feats that Rosini has mastered is the "Thumb Tie" in which he passes his tied thumbs through solid objects, letting spectators examine the knots at will. He performs this amazing illusion today, creating the same sensation as when he first introduced it to the American stage. From India, Rosini also brought the fabulous "Basket Trick" and has presented it not only on the stage but in the center of a nightclub floor, causing a boy to vanish in the very midst of an audience.

One of the most traveled magicians was Milbourne Christopher, who aptly styles himself the "Marco Polo of Magic." While in the service during World War 11, Christopher gave more than a thousand performances of magic, many of them close to the front lines in Europe. His travels have taken him to more than thirty countries, where he has presented magic in the modern trend, specializing in smaller effects which can be readily carried on long journeys, particularly by air.

The phenomenal rise of vaudeville in England, soon after the beginning of the century, attracted many magicians from the States. One was Horace

Goldin who introduced a silent, rapid-fire act in which a dozen illusions were performed in nearly as many minutes. Later, Goldin branched into the full-evening field, and returning to America, devised a "Sawing a Lady" illusion that swept the vaudeville circuits so rapidly that extra units were formed to meet the demand.

Even more unusual was the career of Billy Robinson, stage manager for Herrmann the Great, who devised his own vaudeville act a few years after the maestro's death. Robinson observed that the public was much intrigued by Ching Ling Foo, a Chinese magician then touring the world. Converting his American illusions into Chinese settings, Robinson billed himself as Ching Ling Soo and was an instantaneous success. By the time the public learned that this now Chinese wonderworker was really an American, Robinson was so well established that he continued to appear as Chung Ling Soo until his death.

Another performer who sprang to fame in that lush period was Harry Houdini, whose career is something of an enigma when considered in terms of magic. Houdini set London agog over his highly publicized escape act and for some fifteen years specialized in that type of work almost exclusively. Escapes had been presented by magicians long before Houdini's time and an American performer named Brindamour was quite successful in this field at the time when Houdini began crashing headlines abroad.

132

Brindamour followed the Herrmann style, presenting his escapes in a polished, mystical manner; whereas Houdini turned the act into a challenge. Houdini met with strong competition which he did his utmost to drive out or discourage. Probably his greatest rival was an escape artist named Bob Cunning, who turned to other fields when escape work began to lose its sensational appeal.

During the years in which he rose to fame, Houdini was not rewarded by the public as a magician, but rather as a man of mystery who might be anything from a contortionist to a stunt artist. Done mostly in closed cabinets, escapes created great audience suspense but were puzzling more than magical. Houdini was unparalleled as a showman, but some of his magic was comparatively mediocre, a fact which must be stated in justice to the contemporary performers whose names have been mentioned.

Turning to magic after the escape field waned, Houdini presented single illusions during different seasons at the New York Hippodrome, being featured with the huge extravaganzas that appeared there. Later he entered the lecture field, attacking fraudulent mediums. Gaining tremendous publicity, he started out with his own show, presenting magic and illusions followed by a spook expose. Houdini was hardly into his second season when his untimely death occurred on October 31, 1926.

Houdini's magic show was inherited by his brother, Theo Hardeen who trimmed it to a vaudeville act and performed the choicest of its effects and illusions for nearly twenty years. Since Hardeen's death, some of the Houdini magic has been presented by his former assistant, Douglas Geoffrey, appearing as Hardeen Junior.

It was during Houdini's early surge to fame that he called upon his younger brother to adopt the name of Hardeen and fill added engagements. Presenting escapes in the same style as Houdini, Hardeen was booked solidly for years on the British vaudeville circuits. Later he returned to America and played vaudeville in friendly competition with Houdini. Time and again, Hardeen matched Houdini's stunt of jumping handcuffed from high bridges, making his escape under water.

Both as an escape artist and a magician, Hardeen duplicated much of Houdini's work, yet today the fame of Houdini is more exaggerated than ever. From this it may be concluded that the alchemy of time can transmute gross publicity into golden legend.

Despite the grand scale performances and widespread fame of American magicians, the happy land of magic's high development has been England. For years, London had its own magical theatre, St. George's Hall, once under the joint management of Maskelyne and Devant, two names to conjure with. John Nevil Maskelyne was one of the great inventive geniuses of magic, and members of his family continued his work in the development and presentation of the art.

David Devant held top rating among British illusionists, whose names and creations would require a chapter in themselves. Some of the finest illusions which American magicians rendered famous through their performances were of British origin. In England, magicians gained great popularity on the variety stage. In that country, too, interest in amateur performances and magic as a hobby had an earlier start than in America, which accounts in no small measure for the development of new effects to please a discriminating public.

The top traveling magician of the 1930's. is undoubtedly David Copperfield. He has been seen on TV and in person by more people than any other magician, living or dead. He has combined illusions with other forms of magic and staging to present his full evening show. Other top illusionists of today include Siegfried & Roy, Lance Burton, The Pendragons, and Harry Blackstone Jr.

1. Film to life

Though the illusion of "Film-to-Life" has been rated as the greatest unsolved mystery of modern magic, it does not deserve such an extravagant claim. It is nevertheless a unique stage effect and captured public interest from the day it was introduced. Shown by Horace Goldin during a world tour, it was later adapted and presented by Howard Thurston during an entire season. Few other magicians have used it, due to the complications of production. As a result its secret is comparatively little known.

Effect: A movie screen about ten feet square is lowered to the stage and the magician, standing slightly to the side, introduces "Film-to-Life." A scene is projected on the screen, showing a garden; when the magician claps his hands, a girl appears in the picture, which is scaled exactly to life size. The magician bows to the girl and invites her to sit down, but she gestures that she has no chair. A clap of the magician's hands and a chair appears beside the girl in the picture, much to her amazement.

As the girl starts to sit down, she drops a handkerchief. Before she can pick it up, the magician stoops toward the screen and plucks the handkerchief right out of the picture. Showing it both to the film girl and the audience, the magician rolls the handkerchief and tosses it into the film where the girl catches it. The magician then brings out a cigarette case and offers the girl a smoke. She nods; he holds the cigarette case to the screen. The girl plucks a cigarette from the case. The magician takes one for himself. The girl then gestures that she needs a light, so the magician flicks a lighter, holds its flame to the screen and lights the girl's cigarette. Lighting a cigarette himself, he steps to the side of the screen and suddenly arrives in the picture with the girl. There the magician performs a few magical effects and walks out again upon the stage, coming from the side of the screen. He then invites the girl to join him; stepping to the very center of the stage, he extends his hand, the girl steps forward from the film and as the stage lights suddenly come up, the girl emerges from the motion picture, which ends as she walks to the footlights holding the magician's hand.

Method: Though the effect is intriguing throughout, its mysteries are comparatively minor until the climax. The film of course is specially photographed and later rehearsed accordingly. The plucking of the handkerchief from the film is simply clever palming on the magician's part. During the taking of the film at that point, the handkerchief was removed from the picture. Hence when the magician displays a real handkerchief that he has apparently taken from the screen, the one in the picture is gone.

Similarly, the tossing of the handkerchief into the picture—a very neat effect—is actually the vanish of a handkerchief on the magician's part, timed to the girl's catching of a handkerchief through trick photography used in the taking of the film. The proffering of a cigarette and light are also matters of timing, but this combination of real life with reel has a very baffling effect upon the audience.

The magician walks into the picture by stepping through a slit in the curtained frame that borders it at sides and top. The border looks quite solid and the darkness at the edge of the screen aids in the illusion. The magician's sudden appearance in the picture is timed so neatly that he actually appears to merge into the film. Similarly, his reappearance from the slit in the border is very effective. The sheer novelty of the whole presentation captures the imagination and has the audience believing such things happen.

The screen is affixed to two vertical rollers set in the borders at the side, like a double-ended window shade. It has a few feet of extra length which enables its center to be doubled back, forming a tuck or loop behind the center of the screen. All the while the real girl is in this upright pocket which is held in place by a row of tiny snaps. The division of title screen is not noticeable in the reduced light of the film. As the magician reaches for the film girl's hand, the cue is given; the rollers whip in opposite directions, driving the screen taut. The real girl is practically precipitated forward as the pocket straightens out. Simultaneously, bright lights come on and the magician and the actual girl are walking forward in the glare which reveals only the smooth surface of an apparently normal screen.

The cost of producing the film, the necessity of always being the same girl, and the need of the services of a motion-picture operator, plus the fact that the illusion is only for a regular theater stage—all were reasons why "Film-to-Life" belonged strictly to a large vaudeville act or a full evening magic show.

This unusual stage effect belongs more in the realm of hypnotism than magic, so far as its impression on the audience is concerned. When it was presented by Thurston, he introduced it as a demonstration of hypnosis, though the rest of his show consisted entirely of magic. It was good psychology to include such an effect, as Thurston, like other stage magicians, gave quasi-explanations of some of his illusions by attributing them to hypnotic power. Nevertheless, this particular effect could hardly be presented as anything other than a hypnotic experiment.

2. The Girl of Iron

Effect: The performer introduces a girl who he claims is a remarkable hypnotic subject. He makes a few appropriate mesmeric passes and the girl becomes rigid. As she sways, she is caught by two assistants, who place her in a chair, where she remains rigid, staring at the audience.

Lifting the girl's arm, the performer stretches it in a horizontal position, draws back her sleeve and strokes the arm to make it retain its rigidity. He does the same with the other arm, so the girl is sitting with both bare arms stretched to their full length. Then to prove the amazing strength that can be acquired by a hypnotic subject, the performer orders the two assistants to bring on stepladders, which are set at each side of the chair, behind the girl's arms.

Next, each assistant climbs a ladder and from there places one foot, then the other upon an arm of the girl. Both assistants are thus standing upon the rigid arms, without any other support, much to the amazement of the audience, for the girl bears the weight with scarcely a quiver.

After everyone is convinced that this phenomenon is actual, the assistants descend by the ladders. The performer strokes the girl's arms to relax them, awakens her with a few snaps of his fingers. The girl lowers her arms, awakens and steps forward to take a bow as though nothing unusual had happened.

Method: In fact, the trick is nowhere as unusual as it would appear. Due to the mechanical method employed, the girl has only to act the part of a hypnotized subject. The trick depends on the chair. It has a metal framework concealed

136

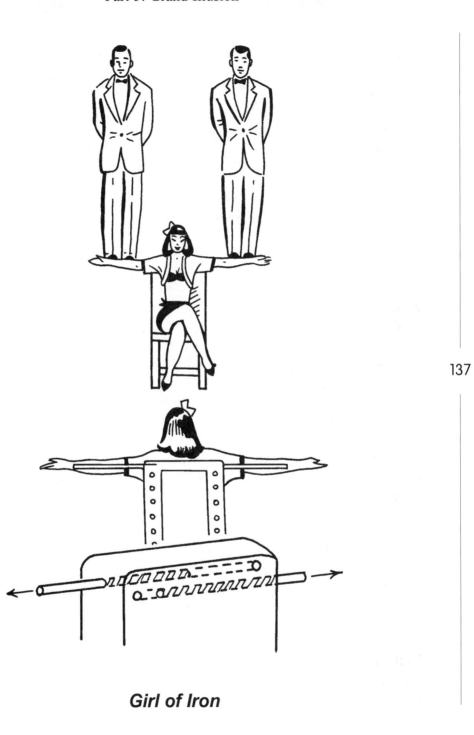

Girl of Iron

in its stout wooden legs, with a vertical bar and a T-brace in its solid back. Metal extension rods are drawn from the T-brace, which runs across the top of the chair back. These extensions are operated in the process of setting and stroking the girl's arms. Hidden behind the girl's arms, the extension rods can not be seen, but it is upon these rods that the assistants place their weight when they apparently step to the girl's arms.

Usually each assistant carries a wooden pole which he uses to take his weight while he is stepping to the extension rods. These poles, extending down to the stage, enable the assistants to gain their balance on the rods. They let the front portions of their feet rest lightly upon the girl's arms and they are then able to lift the poles.

Afterward, the performer, standing behind the chair while he strokes the girl's arms and rearranges her sleeves, is able to push the extension rods into their original position behind the chair back. Thus the "Girl of Iron" turns out to be entirely human, the term "iron" applying only to the chair.

3. The Drop Away Cabinet

Effect: Though this rates as one of the most remarkable illusions ever devised, it has been performed but rarely, due to difficulties in its presentation. The effect is most ambitious. It involves the complete disappearance of a girl from a curtained cabinet that is hanging four feet above the center of the stage and surrounded by a committee from the audience. In a flash, the curtains fall, the girl is gone, and everything may be examined by the mystified spectators in whose midst it happened.

The cabinet is about seven feet tall and four feet square. Its curtains are made of a heavy material, preferably velvet. The cabinet consists of a flat top, a thin floor, connected by four upright corner rods. Near the top of this skeleton affair are horizontal rods from which the curtains are hung. When a cord is drawn, the curtains are automatically and simultaneously released. First the girl enters the cabinet. It is then drawn upward by a chain. Not until the committee surrounds the suspended cabinet are the curtains closed. Then, at the magician's pistol shot, the curtains drop and flatten on the stage, showing the skeleton cabinet empty. The curtains are spread out to show that the girl is not concealed among them.

CURTAINS DROP

SPRING HINGE SPRING HINGE

The Drop Away Cabinet

Method: The method requires two traps: one in the cabinet, the other in the stage directly beneath it. The trap in the cabinet floor consists of two simple flaps that hinge downward, then are sprung back up by springs, so that they lock neatly together. The flaps, however, are not locked at the outset; or should they be so arranged, the girl's weight is sufficient to release them.

When the girl enters the cabinet, she sets her feet apart so that she is standing on a narrow frame that surrounds the flaps. The curtains are then closed around her and at the pistol shot, the girl puts her weight on the trap and drops right through at the instant the curtains drop. At the same moment, the stage trap is opened. It too is of the downward flap variety. Properly timed, the stage trap should be opened a split-second after the girl starts her fall along with the surrounding curtains. The girl continues right through the stage and the heavy curtains, coiling as they land, cover the open stage trap.

By then the trap in the cabinet floor has sprung up and locked. There is sufficient time before the curtains are gathered for the stage trap to close upward and be bolted in place from below. Thus when the curtains are spread for examination the stage is to all appearances, solid. The trap must be finely made and disguised by its carpeting, but the magician steps over it when the curtains are gathered and the cabinet is swung forward for examination.

The problem with this illusion is the perfect timing of the traps, which demands such exactitude that few magicians have cared to perform it. If the stage trap opens too soon, it will disclose the secret; too late, the girl will stop short with the curtains and flounder the rest of the way through. Hence the illusion has only been shown under ideal conditions and after long rehearsal. Not too many modern stages still have trap doors. A special set of stairs with a trap door is commonly used today with a trap door at its top. The assistant simply slides out the trap door in the box and into a trap door at the top of the stairs.

4. The Escape from Sing Sing

This illusion combines the exciting and dramatic effects that place it in the sensational class and add much to its mystery. Originally featured by the Great Herrmann, it has been extensively copied and various other illusions have since utilized certain of its elements. Most of all it has the fast motion which blend surprise and bewilderment, where the audience is concerned.

Effect: On the stage, which is set to represent the interior of a prison, stand two large cages, resembling cells. These cells are upright, each being more than six feet high and measuring about four feet square. The cells are mounted upon platforms; their front doors are hinged. The sides of each cell are provided with roller blinds which form a bright contrast to the steel-gray bars. These blinds may be drawn down when required.

The cells are set well back and a considerable distance apart, allowing space on the center of the stage for the action which rapidly takes place. As the magician is about to introduce the illusion, a convict with striped prison uniform comes rushing on stage, brandishing a revolver. The magician grapples with him, flings him bodily into the cage on the right, clangs the door shut and pulls down the blinds.

Immediately a rattling takes place inside the cage, its front blind snaps up and instead of the convict, the audience sees a man in uniform (the warden), clamoring for release. Hardly has the magician let the warden from the cell, when a revolver shot is heard from the audience and down the aisle races the vanished convict. He rushes up on the stage, apparently seeking revenge, but this time the warden joins the magician in capturing the dangerous prisoner.

This time they put him in the cell on the left, on the assumption that he will be safer there. The blinds are pulled down on both cages and the magician, using the gun that he has wrested from the convict, tops off the drama with sheer wizardry. He fires at the cell on the left, its curtains are released, and again the convict has vanished. The curtains are released around the cell on the right and the convict has mysteriously arrived there. Releasing the bewildered prisoner, the magician turns him over to the warden, who marches him off stage while the magician steps forward to take a bow.

Method: One warden, two convicts, and a pair of special cells are the requirements for this illusion. The cells have loose upright bars at the back which can be quickly removed and replaced. These are masked by special curtains of the same gray as the cell bars and the prison scene. Looking through the front bars of the cell, the audience cannot detect that the back is actually solid (curtained), because so many bars intervene.

The warden is planted behind the cell at the right, where he stands on the ledge of the platform. The first convict rushes on stage, is hurriedly shoved into the cell by the magician. As soon as the curtains are lowered, the convict

141

changes places with the warden, who immediately begins rattling the bars for release. Before the audience can guess where the convict went, his double comes charging down the aisle.

Supposedly the first convict, this man is placed in the cell on the left, where he goes through to the back the moment the curtains are drawn and is hidden there, when they fly up again. Meanwhile, the first convict steps into the cell on the right and appears there when the curtains are raised.

The speed of action and the conspicuous costume of the convict draws suspicion from the fact that doubles are used. The intersection of the warden as a character in the scene is an added factor that does much to confuse the audience. This illusion, however, requires precision as well as rapidity to make it a strong mystery.

The double who appears in the audience goes around to the front of the theater just about the time the illusion begins, rather than be seen there early. Once when Billy Robinson (later Chung Ling Soo) was playing the duplicate convict for Herrmann, he was a trifle late and had to rush to get to the front of the house. On the way, he was spotted by a passing patrolman who mistook him for a real convict, arrested him and put him in jail. During that show, the "convict" never did reappear from the audience and was not located until the next morning.

Blackstone experienced a similar episode when performing an illusion in which an assistant did a quick "run around" and came in from the audience. His assistant mistook the lobby of a movie house for Blackstone's theater, burst into an audience that was watching a Western picture, fired a gun three times and shouted "Here I am!" That took a lot of explanation, but the assistant finally was guided to the right theater, where he made a much belated reappearance.

5. Spiked Alive

Effect: A girl stands in an upright cabinet, large enough to receive her comfortably but with comparatively little room to spare. Above the girl is a square block of wood, from which dozens of long spikes project downward. This block has four handles, two to a side, projecting through slits cut in the opposite sides of the cabinet. The door of the cabinet is closed and two brawny assistants seize the projecting handles of the spiked block. Slowly they draw the handles downward, clear to the bottom of the cabinet, where the spikes make their appearance through the floor of the platform on which the cabinet stands. Apparently the spikes have completely penetrated the hapless girl, but when the spiked block is shoved up to the top of the cabinet again, the door opens and the girl steps out, smiling, at her terrible experience.

Method: This is a very convincing illusion because the spiked block can be slid up and down beforehand to show that it actually operates in formidable fashion. Furthermore, a ribbon can be tied to one of the spikes and the ribbon will come out through the platform, proving that it is the same spike. Nevertheless, all such mysteries have a solution and this one, though deceptive, is comparatively simple.

The whole center of the block is a separate square that simply fits in the outer rim, or frame. This square stays in place by its own weight, its sides being cut at a slightly inward angle. Thus the whole block moves up and down under ordinary conditions, but when the girl is in the cabinet, she has only to place her hands between the center spikes and hold the center of the block, whereupon only the outer frame and its row of spikes will descend when the handles are drawn downward.

The frame is large enough to go around the girl. When it reaches the bottom of the cabinet, its spikes come out through holes in the platform. In the platform is a thin square of metal or wood, provided with spires to account for those in the center of the block. This square is held up by springs inside the platform, which has a double bottom.

Tiny posts or flanges inside the cabinet, at the corners, are engaged by the descending frame. These control the slab hidden in the platform, with its short spikes. Thus the secret slab descends with the frame and pushes the proper number of extra spikes into sight below the platform. When the frame is pushed upward, the hidden square rises with it, bringing the fake spikes up into the platform. The assistants continue upward with the frame and when it reaches the top of the cabinet, it gathers the spiked square that the girl is holding there. This brings everything back to its original status.

The business of the ribbon attached to a spike is simply explained by the fact that it is tied to one of the spikes in the outer frame, hence it actually comes down through the platform with the spike.

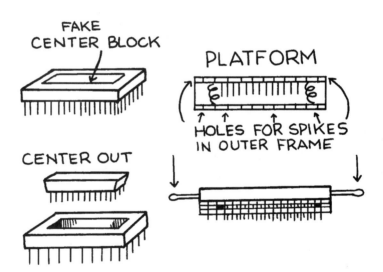

FAKE
CENTER BLOCK

PLATFORM

HOLES FOR SPIKES
IN OUTER FRAME

CENTER OUT

Spiked Alive

6. The Glass Sheet Mystery

Originally planned by Houdini, this illusion was never presented in his show, but later it was built and successfully performed, exactly as designed. Though in effect it is another form of a "Vanishing Lady" illusion, this mystery meets the most exacting conditions. Not only is the girl vanished from a sheet of plate glass; it can be done with the audience on all sides and even performed "in the middle of a thoroughfare" as Houdini himself specified to the author of this book.

Effect: Four assistants clad in Oriental regalia are holding a sheet of plate glass. All the assistants are facing the same direction; two at the front corners, two at the back. The girl is placed on the sheet of glass, which is held flat; a cloth is spread over her by the magician. Suddenly, the magician whisks the cloth away and the girl is gone.

Immediately the four Oriental assistants march away with the sheet of glass, leaving only an empty cloth and a much perplexed audience.

Method: The illusion itself is quite ingenious and worthy of the claims made for it, though if performed out of doors, the setting would have to be arranged beforehand. The cloth used must be a large one, so that it drapes well over the sides of the glass, which is just about long enough to receive the girl. Ordinarily, the magician and an assistant simply spread the cloth full width before draping it over the girl; but if observers are on all sides, the cloth must be specially prepared to retain its shape while the girl is making a quick departure.

That still leaves the question: Where does the girl go? The answer involves the Oriental assistants, in particular one of them, who really doesn't exist. Of the four assistants, only three are real. The fourth, the figure standing at the front of the glass on the side away from the audience, is a dummy figure, entirely hollow. This is the reason for the Oriental regalia, aided by bearded faces, so the dummy looks precisely like the three real assistants.

The back of the dummy figure is open, hidden by the loose-fitting tunic which the figure wears. As soon as the girl is hidden by the cloth, she works her way feet first down into the dummy figure, raising the back of the tunic so she can work her head and shoulders up into the dummy.

145

There is no reason for the girl to slide her hand down into the dummy's arm, for the figure is attached to the glass sheet and the real assistant at the front is holding up the glass. But as soon as the girl is standing in the dummy's legs, the magician yanks away the cloth and the Oriental assistant's depart, the girl walking off inside the dummy.

A slow, impressive march and the effect is perfect. The dummy now is real, so far as its action is concerned and can not be distinguished from the genuine assistant's. Having no reason to suspect that one of the glass carriers is a dummy, the audience is thoroughly baffled by the girl's mysterious disappearance.

7. Crushing a Girl

Effect: Introduced by Thurston, this illusion belongs in the "torture" class of stage magic. On a raised platform stands an oblong box with two doors that are lowered in the front, spaced several inches apart. This box, which has no top, is more than large enough to hold a girl, who enters the box and reclines there. In with the girl are placed a dozen inflated toy balloons, which serve a surprising purpose later.

Another box is introduced, slightly smaller than the first. This oblong box likewise has two front doors; also a similar pair of doors in its top. Thus it resembles two square boxes fashioned into one. Two girls enter this box, one in each side, from the top. The front doors are opened, showing the girls in seated positions, due to the limited size of the compartments. The front doors of this box are closed, but the top doors remain open or are removed, because the heads and shoulders of the girls emerge from the top of the box.

The box containing the two girls is hoisted by chains until it hovers above the larger box that holds the reclining girl. The doors of the larger box are closed. Then, slowly, impressively, the chains are released so that the smaller box, with its double weight, descends into the lower, threatening the welfare of the girl reposing therein.

Since she has no way of escape, the girl in the lower box is threatened by a crushing doom. This becomes more imminent as the upper box sinks 'into the lower. Proving that the fateful moment is nigh, balloons begin to burst, muffled but audibly, until the smaller box has settled entirely within the lower, completely filling it.

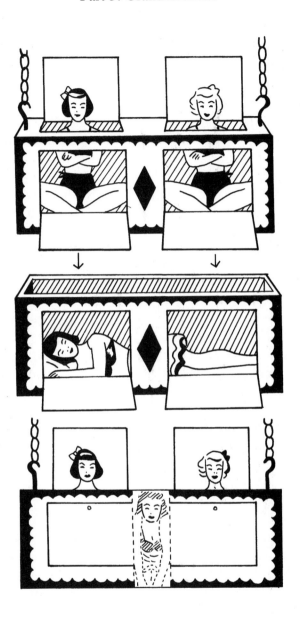

Crushing a Girl

Assistants open the front doors of the boxes. Inside are seen the two girls seated in the smaller box. The girl who occupied the lower box is gone; by magician's logic she has been crushed between the floors of the two boxes. The doors are closed again, the smaller box is hoisted from the larger. When the doors are reopened, there is the girl reclining as calmly as ever, thoroughly recuperated from her crushing experience.

Method: This illusion is accomplished through an ingenious construction of the upper box. Its two sections are divided by a pair of partitions, with a space between, running from front to back of the box. These partitions are like side walls of each section, very close to the edge of each door. However, the partitions are not seen, because the girls are in the box when the doors are opened and they crowd over, hiding the walls beside them.

The space between the partitions is bottomless. Hence the girl in the lower box has only to take a position on hands and knees, facing forward in the exact center of the box; then, when the upper box descends, the hollow space slides over the girl, its walls and top surrounding her like a shell.

The girl lets the balloons remain loose; hence they pop as the smaller box settles into place, giving the "crushing" an authentic touch. After the doors of the boxes have been opened, closed, and the smaller box hoisted, the girl in the larger box resumes her reclining position, giving the impression that she almost fills the box, thus minimizing the size of the space in which she was temporarily crouched.

148

8. The Cane Cabinet

Both baffling and convincing, this illusion forms an interesting variation from the usual form of "torture tricks" in which a young lady proves herself impervious to sinister methods designed for her destruction.

Effect: On the stage is a cabinet mounted on a thin platform so that everyone can see beneath it. The cabinet consists simply of two doors, front and back, side walls and a hinged top that opens upward. Doors and sides are bored with holes, set at regular intervals, in rows.

A young lady enters the cabinet and fills it rather plentifully. The doors are closed, the cabinet is wheeled around, and the magician and his assistants then begin to thrust long canes through the doors and walls of the cabinet, the ends of the canes emerging from the opposite door or side.

Dozens of canes are used, the exact number being immaterial, except that the canes must be abundant enough to prove that the girl cannot possibly squeeze between them. Hence when canes have been thrust through all the holes, the cabinet fairly bristles with the walking sticks, convincing all the spectators that there is not as much as a square foot of space in which the girl could compress herself. The only answer therefore is that a considerable number of the canes must have been thrust through the girl's body.

Then comes the question of the girl's welfare or survival, which the magician promptly settles to the satisfaction of the breathless audience. The canes are all pulled away and flung to the floor. A door of the cabinet is opened and the girl steps out, quite unharmed. Or if the magician prefers to make the climax of the illusion more rapid, a rope can be let down from above, the top of the cabinet opened, and the girl drawn upward clinging to the rope, thus coming clear of all the penetrating canes.

Method: The cane cabinet is a most ingenious device, its great feature being its complete lack of all complications. The canes are genuine and there is no trick whatever about the cabinet itself. The top is of ornamental construction, taking up some six inches or more of space, which looks trivial in proportion to the full height of the cabinet. Furthermore, the uppermost row of holes is several inches below the top proper. Thus the girl can cram herself safely in the least suspected portion of the cabinet, the top.

How does the girl reach the top? The answer discloses the full ingenuity of the illusion. The canes are all thrust into the cabinet in regular order, starting from the bottom and going upward. All the girl does is climb the canes as she would a ladder, pressing her hands against the sides of the cabinet to steady her ascent. By the time the final canes are thrust through the holes, the girl is compactly perched in her unsuspected hiding place.

If the canes are removed so that the girl can step from the door, she has only to descend while the canes are being pulled out from the top of the cabinet to the bottom. If the girl is hauled out by a rope, she simply comes up head and shoulders first. In this case, the hinged top should swing toward the audience, so that spectators in a balcony cannot look into the cabinet while the girl emerges.

9. Catching a Bullet

This celebrated mystery has been performed by a variety of methods, any of which may prove fatal. In nearly every version, the effect is essentially the same. A bullet is marked, then loaded into a gun which is fired point-blank at the magician, who is holding a plate in front of him. The magician coolly catches the bullet between his teeth, drops it on the plate and extends it to the man who marked the bullet, so that it can be identified.

In an obscure book on magic compiled shortly before the year 1800, Philip Astley of London credits himself with the invention of "Bullet Catching," claiming that he devised it in order that a foolish duel between two British army officers would be taught with blank guns. Yet in the years that followed, more than a dozen fatal accidents were recorded among magicians whose precautions failed them during the performance of the trick.

Professor Anderson, the Scottish magician who styled himself the "Wizard of the North" a century ago, performed the trick perhaps a few thousand tines without experiencing harm. His playbills term it "The Gun Delusion" and challenge the audience in so many words to "Bring your own gun." One of Anderson's methods was to switch the marked bullet for an amalgam imitation which dissipated itself when fired from the gun. Once, it is said, a spectator refused to let Anderson handle the bullet and loaded the genuine article in the gun. Anderson challenged him to go ahead and fire, figuring that the man knew the secret and would lose his nerve, which he did.

Considering the fatalities that had occurred with other magicians, the Wizard was taking a long chance on that occasion, trusting in a spectator's whim. Herrmann the Great, who performed the "Bullet Catching" a generation or more later, left the actual shooting to a group of his assistants who appeared as a squad of soldiers. Several bullets were marked, then switched by the captain of the squad, cartridges and all. The bullets fired were of wax and while the squad was lining up, Herrmann obtained the real bullets which were extracted from the cartridges offstage.

The Herrmann presentation was highly spectacular, for on occasion he had the firing squad stand on a platform over the center of the audience, aiming their rifles at the magician on the stage. Though the friendly marksmen never scored a hit on Herrmann, the method was not foolproof enough for his chief assistant, Billy Robinson, who later became the pretended Chinese magician, Chung Ling Soo. Robinson used an old muzzle-loading rifle which had been converted to the breech-loading type. The real bullet dropped down through the breech into the disused ramrod barrel and the magician caught a duplicate. In 1918, when Robinson was performing in Chinese costume on the stage of a London variety theater, the charge fired both barrels and he was killed.

The preferred method of "Bullet Catching" is a one-man version which can be worked anywhere. The secret is little known because so few magicians have been willing to risk its performance and it seems well established that even Houdini, though noted for his daredevil challenges, avoided the bullet trick. The trick is worked with an old-fashioned muzzle-loading pistol which can be fired by a percussion cap and is presented as follows:

Effect: The magician gives a bullet to be marked, preferably with knife-scratches. He lets the pistol be examined, then pours a charge of powder into its muzzle. Next, paper wadding is inserted and tamped down with a short, ornamental ramrod the size of the gun barrel. The ramrod is decorated with circular grooves that appear at regular intervals around its circumference.

In his hand, the magician has a short tube, open at one end, which exactly matches the metal of the ramrod. After letting some person tamp down the powder wadding, the magician takes the pistol by the muzzle and with the handle pointing down, he secretly drops the little tube into the gun, so that it lands with its opening upward. The bullet is next dropped into the muzzle and it falls into the tube. Taking the ramrod, the magician goes through the motions of ramming the bullet home. The gun is given to an assistant who fires it at the magician. Although the magician is thrust backward by the force of the bullet, he manages to catch it in his mouth.

Method: Actually, the ramrod picks up the tube, which stops even with the first concentric circle. Thus the bullet is extracted with the ramrod, which has gained a few inches in length, though this is never noticed. The magician now uses the other end of the ramrod to tamp home another supply of wadding. Leaving the gun in a spectator's possession, the magician takes his distance of say twenty paces, carrying the ramrod with him. While his back is turned, he pulls the tube from the end of the ramrod, obtains the bullet and slips it in his mouth while stooping to pick up a plate from a table. Pocketing the little metal tube, he holds the plate in front of him, faces the gun, and orders the spectator to fire it. There is a report, the magician shows the bullet between his teeth, and the trick is as good as finished.

Not only does this method dispense with assistants who might become careless; the performer faces a gun that has a blank charge and can check the fact because he has extracted the bullet. If for any reason the little tube should prove empty, the magician can call off the trick. Nevertheless, the method is not foolproof. There is still a chance that somebody might drop some other missive into the pistol. On this account, some performers have used an assistant to handle and fire the gun after it has presumably been loaded.

Because of its danger—or at least the threat of such—"Bullet Catching" is scarcely ever performed today. It has been done on special occasions using a model rifle, with firearms identification experts present to confirm the markings on the bullet. But the jinx that holds over it has caused professional magicians to become too wary to include the "Bullet Catching" illusion in their regular performances.

This trick is not recommended for anyone to perform, amateur or professional.

Part 6
Historical Magical Effects

1. The Penetrable Card

As an experiment in passing one solid object through another, the magician introduces a giant playing card, measuring about four times the dimension of an ordinary card. Also the magician has a wooden frame, just large enough to receive the card. This looks like a picture frame except that it is of heavier construction. In addition, the frame is fitted with a broad wooden band or crosspiece which runs horizontally across the center.

Inserting the playing card in the frame, the magician shows it front and back, then sets the frame upon a stand, or easel, which has a large base and a skeleton frame attached. The purpose of the skeleton frame is to support the wooden frame that contains the giant playing card. The two frames are about the same size, in terms of outside measurement.

In the center of the crossbar attached to the wooden frame there is a round hole filled with a circle of leather, cut in slits, line the spokes of a wheel. Thus, though the card can be seen above the crossbar and below, its center is obscured, but obviously must be directly behind the hole in the crossbar.

Taking a pencil, the magician pushes it through the center hole. Next he pokes a handkerchief through, then a wand, and finally his finger. Plainly, the center of the giant card must be punctured. But such is not the case. When the magician removes the card from the frame, he shows it to be undamaged and may even pass it for examination.

All this depends upon a rather ingenious arrangement, which mostly concerns the frame. Purposely made over the frame. Purposely made oversize, the frame has a greater width than the space between its top section and the crossbar, which in turn is equal in width to the frame. In the top of the frame is a segment of a playing card, giant size of course, of just the size to fill the space between the frame top and the crossbar.

Similarly, the crossbar hides another segment of a playing card, designed to fill the other gap. When the frame is inverted, these segments slide down from their biding places and give the appearance of the giant card itself.

154

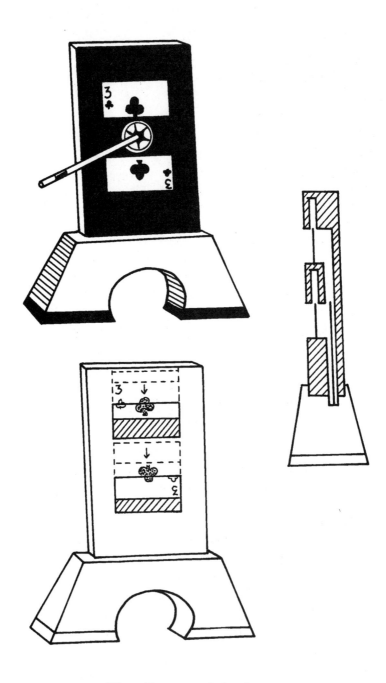

The Penetrable Card

The frame is of double thickness, with a space between. There is an opening at one end, originally the top, but at the other end, the entire frame is solid. When the magician drops the giant card down through the upper slot, it stops, squarely placed in the frame. When he turns the frame around to show the back of the card, he inverts it, but holds the giant card in place.

This causes the two slides to fall into place behind the openings. When the magician turns the frame around again, without inverting it, the false segments are seen, as they are arranged to fall in front of the genuine card,

The easel on which the frame is placed is hollow and has a horizontal slit cut in its top. As soon as he puts the frame on the easel, the magician releases the giant card which drops down into the easel, the top edge of the card coming below the crossbar. Any objects may then be thrust through the hole without encountering the giant card.

At the finish, the magician draws the giant card upward with his fingers until it is again centered in the frame which he then inverts, letting the card fall out while the segments slide back into their original hiding places.

This is one of the most popular-selling magic tricks and is made in plastic and sold as the Penetration Frame.

155

2. The Flowing Coconut

Presented by Thurston as an Oriental mystery, the "Flowing Coconut" formed a surprising stage effect that rivaled the reputed feats of Hindu magic. Actually it surpasses much of the wizardry of India, for the equipment needed for this presentation would not be available to the average Hindu fakir.

On the stage is a huge bowl, mounted on a pedestal. The bowl is filled with water, as the magician demonstrates. He takes the hollow half of a sizable coconut, dips it into the bowl and pours the water from the coconut. This is repeated several times with increasing rapidity until finally the impossible happens.

As the magician makes a quick, sweeping pour from the coconut, the water continues to flow. It gushes downward in a stream which becomes longer and more apparent as the magician raises the bowl higher. Standing with the coconut inverted, the magician causes the mysterious torrent to continue. Not only is the coconut inexhaustible; the huge quantity of water that it delivers soon fills the large bowl and causes it to overflow. A cascade surges over the rim of the bowl and floods a trough around the base of the pedestal. The curtain descends with water still streaming from the coconut, as though its supply were perpetual.

Thurston made quite a spectacle of the coconut trick, but it has been seldom used by other magicians because of the considerable equipment needed for this single feature. The source of the water is a pipe that runs up through the stage, then through the pedestal and finally up through the bowl itself.

This pipe is arranged to deliver a powerful jet of water under high pressure. The coconut has a curved interior to receive the stream. At first, the magician simply dips the coconut in the water which already fills the bowl. In pouring out the water, he inverts the coconut directly over the nozzle of the pipe, which extends to the surface of the water in the bowl.

On the final pour, the coconut is brought almost to the level of the pipe nozzle. That is the cue for an assistant to turn on the water for the pipe, which delivers its full force of water almost instantly. The jet strikes the center of the hollowed coconut, spreads and follows the curve, so that a ring of water gushes downward from just within the coconut's rim.

156

This not only gives the impression that the coconut is delivering as large a stream as a full-fledged firehose; the circle of downward-pouring water serves as a screen for the upward jet that furnishes the actual supply. The real source of the magical gusher is perfectly masked and there seems no possible way in which the coconut could gain so much water, let alone deliver it.

Since the coconut can keep on pouring as long as the city reservoir holds out, this makes a logical finale for a magic show, as the curtain can be lowered and raised time after time, showing the mystery still in operation. Otherwise, the magician simply gives the cue to cut off the jet. The gush of water ceases and he steps forward with the coconut, showing it to be quite ordinary. The magician tosses the amazing coconut to an assistant and proceeds with more marvels. This trick has faded from popularity.

The Flowing Coconut

3. The Imaginary Keg

Famous among feats of magic is the "Inexhaustible Bottle" from which a great quantity of liquid is poured, but such a mystery is quite outdated by the "Imaginary Keg."

In this impossibility, the magician plays entirely upon the imagination of the spectators. He begins by showing a sheet of cardboard, about two feet square, which is embellished with a drawing of a keg. He places the cardboard upon an easel or skeleton stand, then calls attention to the fact that there is a hole near the bottom of the keg, obviously intended for the insertion of a spigot, or tap.

The magician provides such a tap. It is exactly the size of the hole, so he fits it in place. Then he requests the audience to imagine that the keg is a real one. Turning the tap on, the magician provides a flow of liquid that fills a large glass. As the magician hurriedly brings up another glass, it too is filled. More glasses follow until, from the imaginary keg, the magician has filled as many as half a dozen glasses.

Naturally, the liquid must come from somewhere, so the audience supposes that there is a tank behind the cardboard that is resting on the stand. But when the magician removes the tap, be shows that the cardboard is quite innocent of any preparation, while the stand, being of skeleton construction, is equally tree of trickery.

The liquid must come from somewhere in order to flow out of the tap. The place that it comes from is the tap itself. Outwardly the tap appears to be a simple wooden plug, some six inches in length and less than three in diameter. Actually, it is made of thin metal, hence it is quite hollow and contains the liquid which is due to flow from the imaginary keg. When the tap is inserted in the hole in the drawing, a good portion of it goes out of sight, hence the spectators never realize its full size.

This, however, is only half the trick. While the hollow tap contains a surprising amount of liquid, it is scarcely more than enough to fill one of the glasses that the magician uses, provided those glasses were as ordinary as they appear to be.

Special glasses are used. Each has an inner cylinder, sealed at the top. The space between the inner cylinder and the outside of the glass is reduced to less than half an inch. Being of glass or transparent plastic, the inner cylinder is

Imaginary Keg

not visible. Hence when the magician fills a glass, the liquid flows around the inner cylinder. The glass can be shown from all sides, apparently filled with liquid.

The special glasses so reduce the amount of liquid required in proportion to an ordinary glass, that the magician is able to fill half a dozen or more of them from the special tap. This in itself diverts suspicion from the tap, which is removed and laid aside. Then the sheet of cardboard and the skeleton stand may be shown quite freely, leaving the observers baffled as to the source of the mysterious flow.

4. Fish from Air

Featured by Chung Ling Soo in an act of Chinese magic, the art of "Aerial Fishing" stands out as a distinct novelty. An audience is always intrigued when a magician performs something extremely unusual, and the fishing trick—by virtue of its effect—most certainly fulfills that qualification. Though other performers, such as Horace Goldin, have also presented this mystery, it is most effective when introduced in an Oriental setting.

Taking a long fishing pole from an assistant, the magician attaches a hook and sinker to the end of the line. Swinging the line out over the audience, he makes a sudden cast and catches a wriggling goldfish on the hook. Rapidly reeling in his catch, the wizard removes the fish from the line and drops it into a bowl of water where it swims about.

Putting another hook on the line, the magician makes another cast and catches a second fish which is also added to the bowl. He repeats this until he has caught as many as half a dozen fish, all from the thin air above the first few rows of the audience, who find themselves staring upward in search of more invisible fish that have somehow been materialized from nowhere.

The "fish" are contained in the sinkers which the magician attaches to his hook. These weights are actually small hollow tubes. In each is a piece of silk cut to the shape of a goldfish and similarly colored. The strips of silk themselves are slightly weighted, and rolled up in the tubes, to which they are attached by cords.

A quick shake of the rod causes a silk "fish" to drop from the tube, unroll, and wiggle lifelike on the line. In the handle of the fishing rod, the magician has some real goldfish, confined in separate compartments supplied with small wet sponges or paper to keep the fish alive. As he catches each fake fish he obtains a real one from the rod handle. Gathering in the line, he detaches the silk and sinker with the hand that contains the real goldfish, which he promptly drops into the bowl, the sinker along with it.

The swimming goldfish catches full attention in the spotlight while the metal tube and the strip of silk sink unnoticed. Baiting the hook again, the magician continues the aerial fishing until he has used up the supply of real fish in the rod handle. The trick gains effect by repetition, particularly as the increasing number of fish in the bowl convinces the audience that they are viewing something marvelous.

Chung Ling Soo used to "explain" the trick to interviewers by telling them that he snagged the mysterious fish from a bowl that was hidden up the copious sleeve of one of his Chinese assistants, Inasmuch as the hook never went near the assistant, the people who thought they had learned the trick were all the more puzzled when they went to see it again.

When Goldin presented the aerial fishing, he varied it somewhat by carrying a large box which bore the printed word "Bait" in big letters. The supposed bait that he took from the box and attached to the hook before each catch was simply the usual bit of tubing containing the silken imitation fish.

5. Houdini's Giant Bowl Mystery

This effect was presented by Houdini at the famous New York Hippodrome during one of the seasons that he appeared there. Worked near the footlights, it was well suited to such a large auditorium. The items used, combined with the effect itself, resulted in a convincing production.

Houdini began by showing a solid sheet of glass set in a metal frame. This he placed on top of a square, ornamental table. Next, he exhibited a huge glass bowl, practically a giant fish bowl, which he placed upon the frame of glass. The bowl was filled with water and therefore could be seen to be devoid of trickery.

Into the water, Houdini poured a concentrated fluid that gave the water the blackness of ink. Dipping his hands into the bowl, he brought out quantities of silk streamers which continued to appear in almost endless array until the stage all about him was strewn with yards upon yards of silk which had to be gathered by assistants.

Though the bowl was filled with liquid, the streamers appeared dry and their source of origin was most mysterious, considering that the bowl was isolated from the table by the intervening glass. As a finale, Houdini gathered a mass of silk and from it produced a live eagle, the only trained bird of its species, which settled on the magician's shoulder.

Typical of much of Houdini's work, the Giant Bowl Mystery depended largely upon showmanship, though the method, despite its basic simplicity, had the necessary elements to puzzle the audience. The table was of the conventional magician's pattern, with velvet-draped top and gold fringe, and though much sturdier than the average, did not appear overly bulky. This table was actually a sort of box, containing the well-packed streamers, which could be reached through a masked opening in the table's top.

The bowl had a hollow center, composed of a large, watertight glass cylinder. It could not be seen inside the bowl due to the refraction of the water. The cylinder was open both at top and bottom and was large enough for the magician to reach down through. The sheet of glass was made to slide in its frame, in the fashion of a drawer, so after the bowl was set upon the frame, the sheet of glass could be drawn back, unnoticed behind the bowl.

Thus, when the water was darkened, Houdini reached down through the bowl and pulled up the silk streamers, which had their ends looped to form a successive line. The quantity of silk was tremendous and made a line showing. This aided in the final production, because while the audience was watching Houdini, one of the assistants, gathering up the silk, had plenty of opportunity to obtain the eagle, which was in a bag located elsewhere.

When the streamers were brought to the magician for a complete display, he released the eagle from within the bundle, thus topping a remarkably]are silk production with an unexpected sequel, giving the impression that the eagle, like the silks, had emerged from the mysterious bowl.

This trick is typical of the large stage magicians of the early twentieth century. Simple to construct, this illusion can be a great opener or closer for any show. The eagle can be replaced with a dog or cat. The finale can even be a bouquet of flowers.

6. Canary and Lightbulb

Taking a canary from a cage, the magician apparently tosses it at a glowing electric light bulb which is in a table lamp. Instantly, the light goes off and the canary is seen inside the glass bulb, which must be removed and broken open to release the bird. The bulb is of the nonfrosted variety, hence the canary's arrival is visible and as sudden as the extinguishing of the light.

Two bulbs are used, one ordinary, the other containing a canary. They are fitted in a double socket, each portion at right angles to the other. The lighted bulb points straight downward, coming in sight beneath the rim of the lampshade, which conceits the bulb with the canary inside.

The socket is on a swivel, operated by a spring the instant a release cord is pulled by an assistant. This causes the lighted bulb to swing up to the horizontal, while the bulb containing the canary swivels down to the vertical, thus replacing the lighted one. A cutoff extinguishes the lighted bulb and it remains hidden beneath the shade, as the canary bulb originally was, but pointing in the opposite direction.

The bulb containing the canary is of course a special type that comes apart, but it is broken open with a hammer to make it seem ordinary. Two canaries are used; the magician merely pretends to take the first from its cage, actually trapping it in a compartment in the cage bottom.

From the mechanical standpoint, the lamp used in this trick is a fine example of magical ingenuity. It was devised an constructed by Carl Brema of Philadelphia, whose son Will has carried on the manufacture of the precision-built apparatus for which his father was famous. The original lamp was made for Horace Goldin and later was featured by Howard Thurston, through a mutual arrangement.

163

7. Fish and Globe

The production of a bowl of goldfish from beneath a cloth is always highly effective during an opening routine, particularly in conjunction with other productions. Since a fish bowl is anything but collapsible, the audience is much impressed when the bowl arrives from nowhere; moreover, upon seeing the bowl, the spectators are inclined to believe other production objects are also solid and bulky.

Originally, goldfish bowls used in productions were small and quite shallow, more in the style of fingerbowls. Such bowls were covered with broad rubber caps and could thus be hidden beneath the coat, held in vertical position. By reaching beneath a cloth, the magician could obtain the bowl,, bring it level, peel away the rubber cover with the cloth and show the bowl.

To make a more sizeable production, a special type of bowl is now used. This bowl is of the familiar globe variety, the sort in which goldfish are usually sold. With the greatest of ease, the wizard reaches beneath a cloth and brings out a fish globe some six inches high and of proportionate diameter. He sets it on the table, letting the fish swim merrily about while he proceeds with further productions.

This globe is not all that it appears to be. It is constructed to give a maximum of display, while occupying a minimum of space. It is only half a globe, as viewed by the audience and even less than that from the magician's viewpoint.

To the front half of a fish globe is added a crosswise partition, forming the back of the half-globe. This partition, however, instead of being straight, is curved, but not as sharply as the front portion of the globe. Thus, viewed from above the "globe" forms a crescent, its convex lines toward the front.

164

The fake globe is made of plastic or celluloid, so that it is transparent and can hold water. Goldfish swim in the narrow space between the two curves. The bottom of the globe is abbreviated, simply connecting the front of the globe with the curved false back. Attached to the rim of the false back is a celluloid tab, which can be hooked down over the magician's vest pocket. Since the back of the globe follows the curve of the performer's body, the globe is readily concealed beneath the coat, showing no betraying bulge.

To produce, the magician's free hand lifts the globe beneath the coat, automatically releasing it. The globe is then brought from beneath the outspread cloth and held on display, care being taken to keep the curved front directly toward the audience, so that the globe appears to be an ordinary one. The bottom of the special globe should be slightly slanted, rising from front to back. Thus the globe can be set on the table and will stand there, adding to its authentic appearance. When the globe is removed by an assistant, he should bundle up the cloth with it, keeping the cloth bundled around the back of the globe, so that the missing portion will not be discovered.

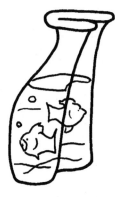

Fish and Globe

8. Aquarium Production

Even more amazing than the production of a fish globe from beneath a cloth, is the appearance of a full-sized aquarium upon a table less than half its height. As with the fish globe, the magician makes this startling production under the cover of a large cloth.

The aquarium looks genuine enough, being of rectangular shape and containing a considerable quantity of goldfish. However, as with many magical properties, its appearance is deceitful. The main portion of the aquarium is simply a thin front, consisting of two walls of glass a few inches apart, closed at the top so the water will not escape. The fish are between these walls of glass.

Hinged at the bottom, this false front lies flat upon the table and springs up when released. The sides of the aquarium are simply flaps of metal, painted to resemble water and goldfish. These spring upward and outward in the same fashion as the front. Underneath the front and sides is a shallow pan of transparent plastic filled with water which can be lifted straight upward from within the table, locking the false front and sides of the aquarium in place.

166

The whole device is covered by a velvet drape which appears to be part of the table top. Under the cloth, the magician pulls away the drape, catches the hidden tray and lifts it, bringing the front and sides of the aquarium upright. He carries the drape away with the cloth and with his free hand splashes some of the water in the tray to prove that the aquarium is as genuine as it appears to be.

The size of the table top is naturally reduced after the appearance of the aquarium, but this only adds to the illusion. It is impossible for the eye to gauge the size or depth of a table top without something by way of comparison. Seen beforehand, the table top looks much smaller than the aquarium, as in fact it is. After the production, it appears to be even smaller and the only object with which it can be compared is the aquarium itself.

Moreover, the actual drape should be gathered under the table beforehand. There it is held in place by little clamps which in turn are connected to the false drape, which the magician removes beneath the cloth. Thus the removal of the false drape releases the genuine one, so that the table top—though smaller and shallower—looks exactly the same after the aquarium has made its magical appearance.

APPENDIX

Magic Shops

Abbot's Magic Company
124 St. Joseph Street
Colon, MI 49040
616-432-3235

All Decked Out
4700 N. 31 Court
Hollywood, FL 33021
954-987-1039

Al's Magic Shop
1012 Vermont Avenue NW
Washington D.C. 20005
202-789-2800

Balloon Box
2416 Ravendale Court
Kissimmee, FL 34758
407-933-8888

Brad Burt's Magic Shop
4204 Convoy St Suite 109
San Diego, CA 92111
619-571-4749

Chaspro Family Fun Shop & Magic Co.
603 East 13th Avenue
Eugene, OR 97401
503-345-0032

Center Stage Costume & Magic
2706 SW 34th Street
Gainsville, FL 32608
352-374-4334

Daytona Magic Shop
136 South Beach St
Daytona Beach, FL 32114
904-252-6767

Denny & Lee Magic Studio
325 S. Marlyn Avenue
Baltimore,MD 21221
410-686-3914

Diamond Magic
515 Lowell Street
Peabody, MA 01960
800-330-2713

Eddie's Novelty & Trick Shop
262 Rio Circle
Decatur, GA 30030

Elmwood Magic & Novelty
507 Elmwood Avenue
Buffalo, NY 14222
716-886-5653

Empire Magic
99 Stratford Lane
Rochester, NY 14612
716-227-9760

Flosso Hormann Magic Co.
45 West 34 Street #608
New York, NY 10001
(212) 279-6079

Hank Lee's Magic Factory
127 South Stree
Boston, MA 02111
781-395-2034

Haines House of Cards
2514 Leslie Avenue
Norwood, OH 45212
513-531-6548

Hollywood Magic Inc.
6614 Hollywood Blvd.
Hollywood, CA 90028
323-464-5610

La Rock's Magic
3847 Rosehaven Drive
Charlotte, NC 28205

L&L Publishing
P.O. Box 100
Tahoma, Ca 96142
800-626-6572

Magic, Inc.
5082 North Lincoln Ave.
Chicago, IL 60625
773-334-2855

Magicland
603 Park Forest Center
Dallas, TX 75234
972-241-9898

Magical Mysteries
4700 N. 31 Ct.
Hollywood, FL 33021
954-987-1039

Meir Yedid
P.O. Box 2566
Fair Lawn, NJ 07410
201-703-1171

Steven's Magic Emporium
2520 East Douglas
Wichita, KS 67214
316-683-9582

Twin Cities Magic & Costume Co.
241 West 7th Street
Saint Paul, MN 55102
612-227-7888

Wizard Craft
P.O. Box 1557
Pleasant Valley, NY 12569
914-635-9379

Publications

GENII
The International Conjuror's Magazine
4200 Wisconsin Avenue, NW
Suite 106-384
Washington , D.C. 20016

MAGIC
**The Independent Magazine
for Magicians**
7380 S. Eastern Avenue
Suite 124-129
Las Vegas, NV 89123
702-798-4893

Summer Camps

West Coast Wizards Camp
PO Box 1360
Claremont, CA 91711
909-625-6194

Tannen's Magic Camp
24 West 25th Street
Second Floor
New York, NY 10010
800-72-MAGIC

Good Places to Visit

There are numerous places where you can find additional information about magicians, magic tricks, and the history of magic. The following are really good places to start:

Library: Your local library may have many books on magic. Look in 793.8 for books on magic, but also look at 793.2 for parties and party games, and 793.87 for juggling.

Book Stores: Usually will offer many titles in their games or hobby sections.

The Internet: There are now hundreds of sites for magicians, magic tricks, and magic shops. A good starting place is http://allmagic.com.

High Schools and Colleges: Many places of learning offer after school or evening courses in magic.

TV Specials: David Copperfield, Lance Burton, and other famous magicians have periodic magic specials on TV.

Science Museums: In certain large cities many of the science museums will teach or have a local magician come to perform.

Travel: Many of the major hotels in Las Vegas have magicians performing in their shows. Some Magician's have their own shows, such as Lance Burton at the Monte Carlo, Sigfried & Roy at the Mirage, and Spellbound, an all magic review at Harrah's. The Boardwalk Holiday Inn features Dixie Dooley's show and a magic museum. Ceasars Palace is where David Copperfied performs when he is in town.

Branson, MO and Atlantic City also offer a wide range of magicians at the various clubs and casinos.

Museums

The Houdini Museum
1433 N. Main
Scranton, PA 18508
570-342-5555

**The Houdini Historical Center
in the Outagamie Museum**
330 East College Avenue
Appleton, WI 54911
920-733-8445

169